FAMILY RECOVERY AND SUBSTANCE ABUSE

HWLCSC
PL

D1065724

For Terri

FAMILY RECOVERY AND SUBSTANCE ABUSE

A Twelve-Step Guide for Treatment

JOSEPH K. NOWINSKI

SAGE Publications
International Educational and Professional Publisher
Thousand Oaks   London   New Delhi

For information:

SAGE Publications, Inc.
2455 Teller Road
Thousand Oaks, California 91320
E-mail: order@sagepub.com

SAGE Publications Ltd.
6 Bonhill Street
London EC2A 4PU
United Kingdom

SAGE Publications India Pvt. Ltd.
M-32 Market
Greater Kailash I
New Delhi 110 048 India

Printed in the United States of America

Library of Congress Cataloging-in-Publication Data

Nowinski, Joseph K.
    Family recovery and substance abuse: A twelve-step guide for treatment / by Joseph K. Nowinski.
        p. cm.
    Includes bibliographical references and index.
    ISBN 0-7619-1110-3 (cloth: acid-free paper)
    ISBN 0-7619-1111-1 (pbk.: acid-free paper)
        1. Substance abuse—Patients—Rehabilitation. 2. Substance abuse—Patients—Family relationships. 3. Twelve-step programs. 4. Family—Mental health. Substance abuse—Treatment.
RC564.N687   1998
616.86/06   21   98-025422

This book is printed on acid-free paper.

99   00   01   02   03   04   05   7   6   5   4   3   2   1

Acquiring Editor:	Margaret Zusky
Editorial Assistant:	Renée Piernot
Production Editor:	Sanford Robinson
Editorial Assistant:	Karen Wiley
Typesetter/Designer:	Lynn Miyata
Indexer:	Will Ragsdale
Cover Designer:	Candice Harman

Contents

Preface

COMMON CLINICAL PROBLEMS posed to practitioners and clinics are requests for help from spouses, partners, and other concerned family members of individuals with alcohol or drug problems. The clinical situation is complicated when the substance abuser is not in treatment. Typically, the concerned significant other is frustrated, at the very least, and may feel hopeless or even desperate.

Chronic substance abuse can have devastating effects on families. Although concerned others are often motivated primarily to get help in persuading the abuser to seek treatment, it is generally recognized that the emotional, spiritual, and physical health of significant others is also seriously compromised by addiction (Collins, Leonard, & Searles, 1990; Paolino & McCrady, 1997). Concerned others have been found, for example, to be significantly stressed (Thomas & Ager, 1993) and to experience greater degrees of depression and physical symptoms, as well as decreased self-confidence, as compared to matched controls (Dominguez, Miller, & Meyers, 1995).

Given the foregoing scenario, the clinician faces a twofold challenge: to respond to the significant other's desire for help in dealing with the substance abuser *and* the need to tend to the mental and physical health of the significant other. In short, the implied therapeutic agenda is complex: indirectly motivating the substance abuser to change while also helping loved ones to change in ways that will improve their own health and well-being.

This book will be useful to both experienced clinicians and those who are training to be clinical social workers, clinical psychologists, family therapists, and substance abuse counselors. The treatment program described here has been used by all of these groups. Experienced clinicians will find it useful in extending their range of clinical competence with respect to the 12-step model of addiction as it pertains to working with family members and other loved ones of substance abusers. Those in training will find it a helpful guide, allowing them to focus treatment.

This treatment program is highly structured and seeks to help the clinician achieve fairly specific and delineated goals. It has been field-tested in clinical trials with significant others of alcohol and drug (Miller & Meyers, 1994, 1996) abusers. Spouses and cohabiting partners, parents, siblings, and other loved ones of substance abusers—including grandparents and adult children—have all been treated using the program described here. It has not been used with minor children of substance abusers. The case examples presented are based on clinical cases drawn largely from these trials, supplemented by the author's own clinical experience.

Broadly speaking, the goals of this intervention are twofold: (a) to improve the well-being of concerned significant others of substance abusers and (b) to teach them how to restructure their relationships to the substance abusers in ways that could enhance the substance abusers' motivation to change.

It goes without saying that the family is a system of interdependent relationships. It is therefore reasonable to assume that any significant change in one member of a family will inevitably change his or her relationships with all others and, therefore, affect the entire family system. In the course of implementing this treatment program, we have found this to be true. That is not to say that other approaches are not effective. The approach presented here, however, is most compatible with the 12-step model of recovery. The treatment protocol itself is presented in manual format in the second half of the book. This will allow the practitioner to use it as a practical guide when working with loved ones of substance abusers. It is intended to be implemented in a brief format (10 to 12 sessions). This may make it particularly useful to those clinicians who must provide care in a managed-care environment in which the allocation of services is closely monitored and contingent on setting specific therapeutic goals and objectives and in which third-party payers advocate the use of mutual-help groups, such as Alcoholics Anonymous and Al-Anon, as adjuncts to formal treatment.

This book is a clinical guide. As such, its focus is pragmatic. It is not a theoretical work, because theory is mainly a concern of social scientists, not of Al-Anon, Nar-Anon, or other 12-step fellowships. If the reader finds this program useful in helping individuals and families begin a process of healthy change and growth, then it will have served its purpose. Similarly, if the assumptions and methods described here are compatible with some theory that the practitioner finds useful, that is fine. This writer, however, will not attempt to superimpose a theory on the 12-step approach for fear that this would most likely reflect personal bias and not the official position of any of the fellowships described here.

Acknowledgments

I would like to acknowledge a number of people whose support and input contributed substantially to this work. Bill Miller and Bob Meyers, of the Center for Alcoholism, Substance Abuse, and Addictions of the University of New Mexico, offered me the opportunity to develop this treatment program for inclusion in their studies of unilateral intervention with significant others of substance abusers. Without that invitation, this program might never have materialized.

I also want to acknowledge how much the work of developing and refining this treatment approach benefited from the input of the skilled therapists who initially implemented it: Rob Anderson, Henry Montgomery, Gary Rudolph, Julie West, and Karla Whetstone. I cannot overstate how much I have learned from observing and talking with them.

My first exposure to the 12-step approach to family recovery took place when I participated in the Family Program at the Hazelden Foundation as a Professional in Residence. I continue to be grateful to the staff of that program for their wisdom and their warmth. It was in that context that I first appreciated the power of caring detachment to change individuals and families.

Barbara McCrady and Patricia Owen were generous in reading a draft of the manuscript and provided very constructive feedback that was incorporated into the final draft.

Last, and once again, I would like to express my appreciation to my editor, Margaret Zusky, for her ongoing support and for staying the course.

PART 1

Principles of Twelve-Step
Family Recovery

CHAPTER 1

Introduction

How It Works

THE FELLOWSHIPS OF AL-ANON and Nar-Anon apply the principles and steps of 12-step recovery as developed originally by Alcoholics Anonymous (AA) and later adopted by Narcotics Anonymous (NA) to concerned significant others[1] of individuals with alcohol or other psychoactive substance use (or both) disorders. This includes spouses or cohabiting partners, parents, children, and other close relations and loved ones of substance abusers. The philosophical connection between Al-Anon and AA is reflected in the fact that the 12 steps that guide each fellowship are identical.

Addiction and codependence are viewed by AA and by Al-Anon as parallel processes characterized by *progressive loss of control* over psychoactive substance use. For the addict or alcoholic,[2] it is use of the actual substance that she or he progressively loses control of; for the codependent, it is the ability to influence the addict's behavior (to get him or her to stop drinking or using) that one loses control over. For the addict and the concerned significant other alike, life becomes increasingly unmanageable as a direct result of substance abuse.

The basic principles that guide the 12-step fellowships of Al-Anon and Nar-Anon are *acceptance* of the loss of control over the substance abuser, *surrender* to some Higher Power as an entity other than individual willpower to place one's hope and faith in, and the *decision* to pursue the 12-step program of personal growth and renewal.

Just as AA states that alcoholics must let go of the illusion that they can successfully and reliably moderate drinking through willpower alone, Al-Anon and Nar-Anon assert that loved ones must also let go of any illusion that they can stop or control another person's drinking or drug use through their own willpower alone. Instead, these fellowships advocate that loved ones modify their own attitudes and behaviors in such ways that the substance abuser comes to make his or her own decision to change. The essence of the Al-Anon message is that the best way to effect change in another is not to coerce, cajole, or threaten the addict, but rather *to change one's own behavior in relation to the addict.* Al-Anon and Nar-Anon could be seen as taking a paradoxical position on change: That fewer efforts to *control* a problem drinker or drug user and more efforts to modify the dynamics of the addict-codependent relationship in the direction of *caring detachment* as described herein is more likely in the long run to lead a substance abuser to come to terms with his or her problem. In its approach to addiction, the 12-step model does much to relieve loved ones of the chronic stress, guilt, and shame associated with feeling responsible for getting a substance abuser to change (and perhaps for having caused the problem in the first place).

In Al-Anon and Nar-Anon, concerned significant others are urged to *detach:* To cease engaging in all those behaviors that (often inadvertently) *enable* the addict to continue using and that, therefore, have the unintended effect of supporting the status quo. A simple rule derives from this advice: By enabling the addict, the codependent unwittingly undermines any motivation for change, whereas through detaching, the codependent enhances motivation for change.

The 12-step model of recovery in some respects parallels what psychologists have called a *decisional* or *transtheoretical* model of change (Prochaska, DiClemente, & Norcross, 1992). According to this theory, behavioral change is dependent on circumstances becoming uncomfortable enough for the individual first to perceive cause-effect relationships (e.g., between drinking and negative consequences), then to make a decision to change, then to take specific action toward changing, and last, to maintain that change. In AA and NA, the addict, by reflecting on the negative consequences of substance abuse on his or her own life (in part through listening to and identifying with others' stories and then telling his own), is helped to gradually move from *denial* of any problem toward *acceptance* that substance abuse has in fact rendered his life increasingly unmanageable. The next step, then, becomes one of *action:* The addict recognizes the need to give up illusions of moderation as a viable goal and to *surrender* instead to abstinence from substance use as a long-term goal and to active participation in the fellowship of AA or NA (or both) as a means to that end.

Within 12-step fellowships, addicts are continually encouraged to turn to spirituality (faith, hope) to maintain motivation in the face of slips or a history of failure and to use the resources within these fellowships for practical advice and support to maintain abstinence "one day at a time." This decisional process is the core theme of all the stories that make up the bulk of the "big books" (AA, 1976; NA, 1985) and that also are a central focus of AA and NA meetings. By going to meetings, listening, and identifying, many addicts have found their way from addiction to recovery. The process through which alcoholics move from denial to acceptance is succinctly summarized in Chapter 8 of *Alcoholics Anonymous* (AA, 1976). In principle, it applies to drug addicts just as well. Although somewhat dated in its language (and unfortunately titled "To Wives," because few AA members were female at the time it was written) it nonetheless describes with remarkable clarity what is essentially a three-stage process that all addicts go through:

- Stage 1: Your husband may be only a heavy drinker. . . . It may be slowing him up mentally and physically, but he does not see it. . . . He is positive he can handle his liquor (pp. 108-109).

- Stage 2: Your husband is showing lack of control. . . . He often gets entirely out of hand when drinking. . . . He admits this is true, but is positive that he will do better (p. 109).

- Stage 3: His friends have slipped away, his home is a near-wreck and he cannot hold a position. He admits he cannot drink like other people, but he does not see why. He clings to the notion that he will yet find a way to do so. He may have come to the point where he desperately wants to stop but cannot (p. 110).

The last stage described—of wanting to stop but being unable to—is the point at which many addicts finally and reluctantly admit to themselves and others that they have a problem. It is only at this point that many make their first appearance at an AA or an NA meeting. This admission—of personal failure over the long run to control alcohol or drug use and the unmanageability that has been the result—is crucial, for it sets the stage for the alcoholic or addict to be open, first, to the need for abstinence and second, to the advice of others on how to achieve it. The primary vehicle for this openness is the stories that the alcoholic or addict hears at meetings.[3]

The key to recovery, then, lies in a willingness to admit to the inadequacy of one's personal willpower in effectively controlling alcohol or drug use and to place one's faith instead in the wisdom and resources of a 12-step fellowship. The format of the personal stories told at AA, NA, and other meetings—how it was, what happened, how it is now—represents what has been called a "core story" (Fowler, 1993) of personal transformation founded on spiritual faith and bonding to the fellowship. It stands as a stark counterpoint to what has been called "radical individualism" (Room, 1993) (or "self-will run riot" as Bill Wilson put it [AA, 1976, p. 62]) in which personal willpower is seen as being more potent than either faith or group support. The core story of AA is a heroic one in contrast to the story of gradual self-immolation that is the story of the addiction process. It is also a story that advocates the strength of fellowship over the strength of individual willpower as a means of achieving and sustaining change.

Storytelling as a tradition and ritual serves to keep the memory of addiction and its consequences from fading and repeatedly affirms each member's decision to surrender to the fellowship and to the 12 steps as a pathway to spiritual renewal and character growth.

Al-Anon and Nar-Anon

Al-Anon and Nar-Anon are based in a belief that letting go of the addict—by learning to detach instead of enabling—is the best way both to motivate the addict to progress through the stages of awareness, decision, and action in the motivational process and to heal the effects that addiction has on loved ones. By enabling the substance abuser, the codependent unwittingly supports the status quo. One common effect of enabling is to insulate the addict from facing the true and natural consequences of his substance abuse. Enabling invariably moderates these consequences and thereby undermines the change process. In contrast, by learning to detach in a caring way, the codependent helps to expose the addict to the true unmanageability of his or her life, thereby promoting change.

Al-Anon can be described as a fellowship that exists for the benefit of the *affected*: for those significant others whose lives—whose mental, spiritual, and physical health—have been affected negatively as a consequence of being in a close relationship with an addict or alcoholic (Al-Anon, 1985). In addition to Al-Anon, which welcomes all those whose lives are affected by alcohol, Alateen is a fellowship specifically for the children of alcoholics. Similarly, Nar-Anon is a fellowship that is open to significant others of drug abusers and addicts.

Despite their implied belief that caring detachment will ultimately prove more successful than enabling in getting alcoholics and addicts sober, all of these fellowships exist first and foremost not so much to motivate addicts as for the support and renewal of loved ones who have been negatively affected by addiction. Depression born of chronic frustration and failure (to get the addict to stop), compounded by feelings of shame or guilt (over possibly being responsible), and anxiety (over what might happen), are some of the emotional and spiritual burdens that are commonly brought to Al-Anon and Nar-Anon. Families typically spiral downward into dysfunction as they unravel in the face of addiction. Al-Anon and Nar-Anon are fellowships where such problems can be openly talked about, where emotional wounds can be healed, and where personal growth can be renewed. *This is so, regardless of whether or not the addict chooses recovery over addiction.*

If AA and NA were founded on the idea that alcoholics and drug addicts must eventually make decisions to stop trying to control their drinking and drugging through willpower and instead, to accept the necessity to abstain along with the advice and support of fellow recovering addicts, then Al-Anon and Nar-Anon represent the complement of this. These fellowships recognize that codependents often need help coming to accept their own powerlessness over the addict and that they also need support in learning to detach as opposed to enabling the addict. Al-Anon and Nar-Anon's primary assumptions are as follows:

Loss of Control: Just as the addict becomes progressively more powerless to effectively moderate drinking or using as he or she moves from social use through habitual use toward eventual compulsive use, so is the codependent progressively more powerless with respect to getting the addict to stop. The codependent cannot prevent the alcoholic from drinking or the addict from using but may not truly accept this fact or its implications for a long time (Al-Anon, 1982, p. 236).

Faith: Because the codependent is in fact powerless (over addiction), she or he needs to "turn over" the fate of the addict to a Higher Power—in effect, to stop efforts to control the behavior of the addict and to shield him or her from negative consequences of use. Instead, according to Al-Anon, codependents need to begin attending to their own health and well-being (Al-Anon, 1982, p. 236). Just as the addict can harbor despair about the chances for success, so can the codependent feel hopeless and helpless. The emphasis on faith within 12-step fellowships relates directly to this problem. Hopelessness undermines motivation to change. Addicts and codependents alike are repeatedly called on, in 12-step fellowships, to have faith and hope. This is the essence of the second step: *Came to believe that a Power greater then ourselves could restore us to sanity.*

Fellowship: The fellowships of Al-Anon and Nar-Anon provide strong and constant sources of comfort, advice, and support to loved ones as well as a vehicle for personal healing and growth through their 12 steps and traditions (Al-Anon, 1985, p. 232).

Detaching: A common wisdom within 12-step fellowships goes like this: "Addicts are sick people, not bad people." The underlying belief expressed here is that addicts typically do not get better merely through being criticized, punished, or rejected. At the same time that the codependent needs to refrain from condemning the addict, she or he must also take concrete steps to stop acting in ways that have the unintended effect of allowing the addict to remain in denial regarding the truth of his or her problem (Al-Anon, 1985, p. 29). *Caring detachment* is consistent with the attitude toward addiction and recovery that is advocated by AA and NA, which states: "We are not responsible for our disease, but we are responsible for our recovery" (NA, 1985, p. 20).

The guiding principles behind Al-Anon and Nar-Anon were set forth initially in Chapter 8 of *Alcoholics Anonymous* (AA, 1976). Written by the wife of a recovering alcoholic, it advocates an approach to dealing with the problem drinker that is reflected in the subsequent publications of Al-Anon and Nar-Anon. This includes admonishing codependents to abandon their efforts to change or shield the addict and turn their attention instead toward their own spiritual, mental, physical, and social well-being.

The frustration of partners of alcoholics is captured poignantly in the following excerpt from Chapter 8 (AA, 1976): "As animals on a treadmill, we have patiently and wearily climbed, falling back in exhaustion after each futile effort to reach solid ground" (p. 107).

By conceptualizing alcoholism as compulsive behavior that has defied all efforts at self-control, Chapter 8 (AA, 1976) suggests that the only "sane" course of action for the codependent is to "let go," to stop protecting the addict: "We never, never try to arrange a man's life so as to shield him from temptation" (AA, 1976, p. 120).

It is apparent how shielding a person from temptation can be dysfunctional. First, it tends to make the codependent, as opposed to the addict, responsible for getting sober. Although some behavioral models of working with significant others do seek to intervene directly on this level (Meyers & Smith, 1995), by and large, this is not the approach advocated within 12-step fellowships. For one thing, they assume that loved ones have already tried, unsuccessfully, numerous times to get the alcoholic or addict to stop.

A second reason not to shield someone from the temptation to use is that this can easily lead to shielding the addict from the negative consequences of use. If AA suggests a way for loved ones to effectively motivate problem drinkers to change, that way could be described as indirect. Consider the following advice (AA, 1976):

- ▓ Lay the groundwork for a friendly talk about his [sic] alcohol problem. . . . Be sure you are not critical during such a discussion. (P. 111)
- ▓ Wait until repeated stumbling convinces him he must act, for the more you hurry him the longer his recovery may be delayed. (P. 113)
- ▓ After his next binge, ask him if he would really like to get over his drinking for good. Do not ask that he do it for you or anyone else. Just would he *like* to? (P. 112)

Such advice is more consistent with subtly encouraging motivation for change through what Al-Anon calls caring detachment than it is with attempting to shape behavioral change through reward or punishment. Both philosophically and practically, AA and Al-Anon are much more compatible with the former than the latter approach.

AA and Al-Anon consistently advise loved ones to resist any temptation to shield the problem drinker or user from the natural consequences of drinking or drug use. Here is an example of the advice AA offers in this regard:

> Frequently, you have felt obliged to tell your husband's employer and his friends that he was sick, when as a matter of fact he was tight. Avoid answering these inquiries as much as you can. Whenever possible, let your husband explain. (AA, 1976, p. 115)

Last, Al-Anon and Nar-Anon, like AA, are strong proponents of spiritual renewal and characterological growth. In fact, some newcomers to Al-Anon or Nar-Anon may be initially dismayed by the *lack* of talk about alcoholics and addicts at some meetings. These meetings may simply have evolved to the point where the emphasis is decidedly on the growth and well-being of the members, as opposed to the status of their drinking or using partners, who are left to be responsible for themselves. As one veteran Al-Anon member, whose husband had been in recovery for 20 years, put it:

> I've always been a real controller. Al-Anon helped me learn how to let others be responsible for themselves. I really think that Al-Anon saved my life, because I was drained, spiritually and physically, from always trying to be in control. That's why I still go meetings regularly—not because my husband drinks, because he doesn't, but just for me.

Al-Anon and Nar-Anon Versus Family Therapy

Family therapy has evolved into a clinical specialty within the mental health professions. Different schools of family therapy view the causes of dysfunction differently; consequently, their approaches to intervention differ. It is important to understand that none of the 12-step fellowships, including Al-Anon and Nar-Anon, which are the main focus here, have any formal connection with family therapy as a discipline. Although one can superimpose a psychological "theory" on how they work, 12-step fellowships espouse no such theories themselves. Rather, they exist and have evolved as mutual-help groups, remaining intentionally nonprofessional (Nowinski, 1998).

All 12-step fellowships are based on the assumption that addiction is a *primary* dysfunction or diagnosis. In other words, they do not regard substance abuse and addiction as symptoms of some other family dysfunction or individual problem. Accordingly, the emphasis in 12-step meetings, from AA to Al-Anon, is on addiction and even more specifically, on individual recovery from addiction, much more so than on any other issue. This means that staying sober will always be the main focus in AA and Al-Anon (although the latter interprets "sobriety" as that term applies to codependents). Once sober, the individual member of a 12-step fellowship is invited to pursue a program of spiritual renewal and character development by "working" the 12 steps in their day-to-day lives.

Al-Anon and Nar-Anon do not regard substance abuse or addiction as symptoms of family dysfunction or personal psychopathology, in the sense that family dysfunction or psychopathology could be said to be *etiological* of substance abuse. On the contrary, they are much more inclined to regard substance abuse and addiction as etiological of other family dysfunctions, from marital conflict, spousal abuse, and poor boundaries to childhood depression and adolescent alienation. Moreover, once the recovery process has begun, members of 12-step fellowships are apt to have faith that many of these other family problems will be able to be successfully resolved.

This perspective on substance abuse, addiction, and its sequelae can be uncomfortable to family therapists who have been trained to detect family dysfunction and to regard it as etiological of addiction. In a sense, the 12-step view challenges family therapists to let go of whatever preconceived notions of etiology they may have learned and to view families and family dysfunction through a different lens—in effect, to entertain the reverse hypothesis. Family therapists wishing to explore this route to family healing are invited to try the methods described here. To do so successfully, however, they must be open to the idea that addiction is the *cause* of spiraling family dysfunction, not a result of it, and also that this spiral can begin to be reversed when even one significant other starts relating to the addicted family member through caring detachment.

From the point of view of Al-Anon and Nar-Anon, then, family recovery is a process that begins when one or more members of a family that has been affected by addiction begin the process of recovery. Specifically, that means taking the first step, which is to ackowledge that one is powerless over another person's addiction (and consequently, not responsible for it) and begins to move from an enabling relationship with the addict toward a relationship characterized by caring detachment. As simple as this may sound, it is no small feat. It also has profound implications for the individual, for the addict-codependent relationship, and indeed, for the whole family. Some of these implications are explored in this text.

Goals and Objectives of the Program

The structured treatment program that is described in detail in Part 2 of this book has specific goals and objectives. These are described in the discussion to follow. The reader should be aware that this treatment protocol is highly focused. Consequently, the same issues are raised repeatedly, and progress toward achieving goals and objectives is monitored continuously. The same issue (e.g., caring detachment) may be approached many times, each time from a slightly different perspective, in an effort to find one or more such perspectives that the client can relate to.

Experience has taught us that it is very easy for even experienced therapists to drift away from the specific goals of the program. At times, it is client resistance that accounts for this drift, because some of the recovery tasks that clients are asked to do between sessions may arouse discomfort or anxiety. Maximum benefit will be achieved when such drifting is minimized. Accordingly, practitioners are encouraged to review the format for sessions in advance and to make every effort to cover the material.

Treatment Goal #1: Active Participation in the Al-Anon or Nar-Anon Fellowship (or both)

Specific Objectives

▦ Attending *meetings*

▦ Getting and using member phone numbers, both in times of crisis and more generally, so as to develop a *network of contacts*

▦ Getting and establishing a relationship with a *sponsor*

▦ Reading and responding to suggested *readings* from fellowship literature

Treatment Goal #2: Caring Detachment

Specific Objectives

▦ Decrease in self-reported enabling behaviors

▦ *Acceptance:* Self-reported acceptance of personal loss of control (powerlessness) over the addict's drinking or using behavior and an expressed willingness to turn over the fate of the addict to a Higher Power.

▦ *Surrender:* An expressed willingness to accept the support and advice of the Al-Anon or Nar-Anon fellowship in one's efforts to resist enabling and to detach, and an expressed faith in some Higher Power.

▦ Increased interest in and commitment to personal growth and development on the part of the significant other (e.g., making new friends, renewed interest in work or personal health, etc.)

▦ Readings and Journaling

Concerned significant others who participate in this program are asked to read specific parts of the following publications: *Al-Anon Faces Alcoholism* (Al-Anon, 1985) and *Alcoholics Anonymous* (AA, 1976). In the case of loved ones of drug users, selected readings from *Narcotics Anonymous* (NA, 1985) may be substituted. Selected pamphlets are also included as recovery tasks.

Clients are also asked to maintain journals in which they record their reactions to readings as well as their reactions to all 12-step meetings they attend. As much as possible, the practitioner should make specific efforts to incorporate journal entries and reactions to readings into the therapeutic dialogue.

Program Overview

The treatment program consists of eight core topics plus a termination session. These can be delivered through individual counseling sessions, or they can be used as topics for a group. Working with groups has the advantage of providing a context in which participants can be encouraged to initially attend meetings together and otherwise network with one another, much the way they are encouraged to network within Al-Anon or Nar-Anon. As discussed earlier, the program can be applied to partners, parents, grandparents, and even adult children of substance abusers. It is important, however, that this person (or persons) have frequent contact with the substance abuser. Clinically, we have found that those seeking treatment are, in general, family members or partners on whom the substance abuser is dependent in one way or another.

The eight core topics of the program are as follows:

Topic #1: Program Introduction & Assessment

Topic #2: Principles of 12-Step Fellowships

Topic #3: Al-Anon or Nar-Anon

Topic #4: Denial

Topic #5: Acceptance

Topic #6: Enabling

Topic #7: Surrender and Getting Active

Topic #8: Detaching

Notes

1. The terms *concerned significant other* and *codependent* are used in this text more or less interchangeably. They refer to any loved one of a substance abuser who has been affected as a result of being in a relationship with that substance abuser. The use of the term *codependent* is not intended to be pejorative in any way. The phrase *concerned significant other* could have been used exclusively but

seemed unwieldy. The term "codependent" does imply some effect of addiction on loved ones, and this is, in fact, what 12-step fellowships assume to be the case. Moreover, the term is commonly used within 12-step fellowships. The author does not, however, wish to endorse any definition of codependence other than what is described herein (i.e., to be in a close relationship with a substance abuser and to therefore be affected by addiction.) The term as used herein is generic and is not intended to imply any specific psychopathology.

2. For purposes of brevity, I will at times use the single term *addict* to refer to alcoholics as well as those addicted to other psychoactive substances.

3. The single term *meeting* is used here to refer to any 12-step fellowship meeting, including AA, NA, Al-Anon, and Nar-Anon.

CHAPTER 2
Al-Anon and Nar-Anon Facilitation and Family Recovery

THE OVERALL GOAL of this treatment program can be thought of as "facilitation." The practitioner seeks to facilitate the gradual involvement of a loved one in a 12-step fellowship for concerned significant others of substance abusers. The therapist also attempts to facilitate the gradual development of a relationship with the substance abuser that is characterized more by caring detachment than by enabling.

The role of the therapist—who could also be called the *facilitator*—as well as the structure of treatment are described in this chapter.

Facilitation can best be thought of as a *collaborative relationship* between a knowledgeable professional (the therapist) and the client. The terms *facilitator* and *facilitation* are used frequently here because they tend to be more descriptive than the traditional ones of *therapist* and *therapy.* In this model, the primary agent of change is thought to be a 12-step fellowship (Al-Anon or Nar-Anon). Through involvement in one of these fellowships, the loved one of an addict receives advice, comfort, and support. In contrast, as family therapy is traditionally conceived, it is the patient-therapist relationship that is seen as the primary agent of change. This perspective on change is not meant to diminish in any way the importance of the therapeutic relationship or to minimize the skills needed by the practitioner to successfully implement this program; rather, the intention is to keep the focus clear as to the primary responsibility of the professional and what will be gained when a client successfully bonds to Al-Anon or Nar-Anon.

Loved ones are clearly and repeatedly encouraged here to establish ongoing relationships on several levels with 12-step fellowships as a means of sustaining change. This is because the facilitator-client relationship is time limited and also, because the facilitator may not be available in times of crisis, whereas other members of these fellowships are.

Role of the Facilitator

The facilitator is a skilled professional who attempts to establish a collaborative relationship with the client, who educates the client with respect to 12-step recovery, and who constructively confronts the client regarding his or her behavior and attitudes relative to the addict as well as the client's own mental and physical health.

The facilitator role has been previously described with respect to facilitating early recovery for persons with alcohol or drug problems or both (Nowinski & Baker, 1998; Nowinski, Baker, & Carroll, 1992). This role is essentially the same with respect to working with the loved ones of substance abusers. Descriptions of its elements follow:

Education and Advocacy

The facilitator acts as a resource and advocate of the 12-step approach to recovery in the following ways:

Explains the AA-NA view of alcoholism or addiction as a chronic progressive disorder marked by loss of control and negative consequences associated with substance use (i.e., "unmanageability")

Helps the client to assess the extent to which alcohol or drug use or both has made the substance abuser's life progressively more unmanageable

Helps the client assess the extent to which the addict's drinking or drug use has made his or her own life progressively more unmanageable

Identifies denial as it is reflected in the addict's attitudes toward drinking or using as well as in the client's attitudes toward the addict's behavior. Denial is viewed as a symbiotic process in which the substance abuser and the significant other each play a role in shielding the addict from the natural consequences of substance abuse and in maintaining the status quo in their relationship

Introduces several key 12-step concepts and helps the client to understand them by identifying specific experiences that illustrate them

Introduces, explains, and advocates reliance on the fellowships of AA-NA and Al-Anon or Nar-Anon for the problem drinker and the significant other, respectively

Explains how to make use of various Al-Anon or Nar-Anon resources

Explains recovery as a process of ongoing process of "arrest" of addiction as opposed to a so-called cure

Explains the role of a sponsor and helps the client to identify what to look for in choosing an initial Al-Anon or Nar-Anon sponsor

Answers questions to the best of his or her ability about material found in AA-NA and Al-Anon or Nar-Anon literature

Guidance and Advice

The facilitator actively and systematically encourages the significant other's involvement in Al-Anon or Nar-Anon in the following ways:

Monitors the significant other's ongoing involvement in Al-Anon or Nar-Anon and encourages a progression toward greater involvement and bonding, for example, by the following:

- Suggesting meetings that require increasing personal involvement, such as so-called step meetings and closed meetings (as opposed to open discussion meetings)

- Encouraging the client to volunteer for basic service work, such as making coffee and either setting up for or cleaning up after meetings

- Encouraging the client to get phone numbers and to call Al-Anon or Nar-Anon friends between meetings

- Assisting the client in locating meetings and providing appropriate support for getting codependents to attend and participate; this can include the following:

  Problem solving around issues such as transportation or child care

  Role-playing how to ask for phone numbers, volunteer for responsibilities, approach a potential sponsor, and so forth

  Role-playing around situations that the client may express anxiety about (e.g., disclosing his or her Al-Anon involvement to the substance abuser)

  Arranging for an active Al-Anon or Nar-Anon volunteer to meet the client and escort him or her to one or two initial meetings

Clarifying the role of an Al-Anon or Nar-Anon sponsor; encouraging and assisting the significant other in finding a sponsor

Suggesting so-called recovery tasks that will enhance the significant other's successful integration into the fellowship of Al-Anon or Nar-Anon

Motivation and Support

The facilitator makes specific efforts to empathize with the significant other and to motivate him or her to use Al-Anon or Nar-Anon by the following:

Demonstrating an empathic understanding of the client's feelings of shame, anger, anxiety, and guilt regarding substance abuse and the unmanageability it has caused

Empathizing with the client's resistance to accepting loss of control over addiction and the need to detach from the addict.

Consistently pointing out the impact of the significant other's behavior on the substance abuser

Treatment Note: Reinforcing Change in Codependents

The facilitator can have a major impact on the significant other's motivation to change the basic dynamics of the addict-codependent relationship. One way to do this is to be alert for and to point out the impact that the significant other's behavior has on the substance abuser. The dynamics of the addict-codependent relationship are usually obvious: The more the codependent stays the same—in other words, the more the addict-codependent relationship remains status quo—the less the addict is inclined to change. Clinical experience teaches us time and time again that even small changes in a significant other's behavior (and consequently in the relationship) cause reactions in the addict. An action as simple as letting the addict know that one is attending Al-Anon, is reading about addiction, or is attending this program, typically causes the addict to react. Not infrequently, drinking or using decreases, at least temporarily. Often, the addict will become defensive—a sign that a change in the relationship has been perceived. Sometimes, the couple begins a dialog about substance abuse, unmanageability, and recovery. By pointing out such effects when they become apparent, the facilitator counters feelings of hopelessness, empowers the significant other, and encourages change.

Desired Facilitator Characteristics

This section describes the knowledge base and some of the characteristics that may contribute to therapeutic effectiveness when using this model. To the extent that a professional possesses or is able to develop these characteristics and knowledge base, she or he may be more effective in using this program.

Knowledge of the Recovery Culture

A facilitator is a professional whose therapeutic goals are fairly complex. The facilitator seeks to promote active participation in Al-Anon or Nar-Anon, to help clients understand key recovery concepts, and to guide clients in their first steps toward caring detachment. To pursue these goals effectively, the practitioner need not necessarily be either a codependent or a recovering addict. It goes without saying, however, that she or he needs to be reasonably knowledgeable of and comfortable with the principles that guide 12-step fellowships. These are described in the steps and traditions of those fellowships.

To be maximally effective, the facilitator should also be familiar with the Al-Anon or Nar-Anon and AA-NA culture as it is reflected in actual meetings. For these reasons, it is important that any professional who is not personally involved in AA-NA or Al-Anon or Nar-Anon, but who is planning to use this manual-guided approach, attend several open meetings prior to using this manual with a client.

In addition, to be effective as a facilitator, the professional using this approach is encouraged to develop a network of Al-Anon or Nar-Anon contacts: men and women who are active in the fellowship of Al-Anon or Nar-Anon and who could be called on to meet a shy or ambivalent client at a first meeting, to provide the facilitator with information about particular meetings, to talk with a client over the phone, and so on. Facilitators can develop working relationships with these people by going to meetings on some regular basis or simply by networking with recovering persons they know.

Treatment Note: The Use of Slogans

Slogans are an integral part of the 12-step recovery culture. The facilitator should be familiar with at least some of these slogans and should introduce them as they are appropriate in treatment. These slogans—"Easy does it," "One day at a time," "Let go and let God," "First things first," and so forth—should never be dismissed as mere clichés. Rather, they represent succinct statements of wisdom that are firmly rooted in many recovering persons' real-life experiences. The book, *Al-Anon Faces Alcoholism*, (Al-Anon, 1985) includes a section that discusses slogans and their meaning (pp. 248-252).

Active, Supportive, and Involved

Facilitators should work toward being active, engaging, empathic, and nonjudgmentally confrontive during sessions (as opposed, for example, to being merely reflective, detached, or overly interpretive). Twelve-step-oriented treatment for substance abuse is often stereotyped as an exceedingly confontational approach whose goal is to "break down" clients' denial; in other words, to confront them until they admit to the problem (Marlatt, Tucker, Donovan, & Vuchinich, 1997). The program presented here is *not* an aggressively confrontational therapy. The facilitator is a source of information and may be quite frank in sharing perceptions, for example, regarding denial or enabling on the part of the significant other. But the facilitator does not lecture or scold clients for their so-called dysfunctional attitudes or behavior, much less aggressively challenge their denial. An effective facilitator endeavors to establish a collaborative, supportive, and honest relationship with the client. As part of this relationship, the facilitator may at times be frank, respectfully sharing an observation even if that observation makes the client uncomfortable. But this is true of any good psychotherapy.

Overall, the goal of the facilitator is to help the significant other to understand and identify denial (i.e., resistance to acceptance) and codependence (i.e., resistance to detaching) as these are revealed in the significant other's decisions, words, and actions in relation to the substance abuser. The facilitator confronts the client consistently in a frank but respectful manner regarding attitudes or behaviors that support drinking or that reflect a lack of understanding of alcoholism or drug addiction, consistently encourages the client to get involved in the fellowships of Al-Anon and or Nar-Anon, and helps the client to understand key Al-Anon or Nar-Anon concepts in terms of his or her experiences with the substance abuser.

Facilitators should appreciate the fact that 12-step concepts allow much room for individual interpretation. Significant others can and should be expected to interpret 12-step concepts in light of their own experiences. What may represent an unmanageable life for one person, for example, may not seem quite so unmanageable when viewed through the eyes of another. What is one person's Higher Power may not be another's. And so on. This pluralism is consistent with 12-step fellowship traditions, which not only allow but also actively encourage individuality of interpretation within broad guidelines. What is most important is not whether two clients each interpret 12-step concepts in precisely the same way; what counts is the end result: acceptance of progressive unmanageability caused by substance abuse and movement toward caring detachment in relation to the substance abuser.

Focused

This program seeks to initiate a process that will lead to significant change in a loved one and his or her relationship to a substance abuser, yet it also seeks to accomplish this within a relatively short period of time.[1] It is consequently highly structured and tightly focused. For each client, it becomes a therapeutic challenge to cover as much ground as possible, given the circumstances of the particular case.

In general, it is expected that all eight topics can be covered in 12 to 14 sessions. To be able to accomplish this, the facilitator needs to be able and willing to focus treatment and to stay on task. Typically, sessions are scheduled weekly, at least initially, partly to establish rapport and partly to initiate involvement in Al-Anon or Nar-Anon. Later on, meeting every other week may be appropriate because it allows more time for attending meetings and other opportunities to bond with the fellowship as opposed to the facilitator.

At the beginning of each session, through the process of reviewing the previous week, issues relevant to the significant other's life can be expected to come up. The client needs to be given time to articulate his or her problems and concerns and to feel heard by the facilitator. At the same time, it's important to keep in mind that the structured nature of this program does not allow facilitators to "follow the client" entirely—in other words, to pursue a client's agenda to the exclusion of the facilitation program's content or objectives. In light of this, it is the facilitator's responsibility to keep sessions focused and to avoid getting into lengthy discussions of other matters (job problems, parenting problems, marital problems, etc.). At such times, the facilitator is advised to invoke the "first things first" principle: Emphasize the client's need to first use the resources of Al-Anon or Nar-Anon, to work on successfully detaching from the addict as a first step toward personal and family recovery, and to defer dealing with other issues until some progress has been made on this. As pointed out earlier, detaching, even in small ways, has clear effects on addicts and on relationships. This may lead to beneficial spillover effects in areas that the client may be concerned with. Some problems, in fact, may resolve more or less spontaneously once the client has altered the addict-codependent relationship by placing his or her own enabling behaviors and attitudes in check. Other problems may persist and require further attention later on. However, except for instances of active spousal or child abuse or severe depression with suicidal ideation, loss of social functioning, or both, most collateral issues can usually be put on hold while the client focuses first on learning to detach and on beginning to bond with Al-Anon or Nar-Anon.

The facilitator needs to give the client two messages consistently and repeatedly. The first is that enabling invariably reduces the substance abuser's motivation for change, whereas caring detachment can promote motivation for change. Second, successful detaching affects the addict-codependent relationship in ways that will ultimately prove healthier for both the substance abuser and the codependent. Once the change process—from enabling to detaching as the primary way of relating to the addict—is established, collateral issues, such as strained marriages and alienated family relations, may be more effectively addressed, perhaps by adding traditional family or marital therapy into the comprehensive treatment plan. Attempting to address them prior to this, however, may not prove fruitful.

For the addict or alcoholic, the first and foremost goal in early recovery is to get active in AA or NA. "Don't drink, and go to meetings" is the advice invariably given to the newcomer. Similarly, significant others can be advised: "Don't enable, and go to meetings." This marks the starting point of not only the recovery for the significant other but also for change in the addict-codependent relationship and in the family.

Treatment Note: Avoiding Distractions

Despite the facilitator's best efforts, some clients may persist in trying to bring the focus of sessions onto some other issue that they regard as more pressing than the one the facilitator wants to discuss. This may reflect denial (of the unmanageability caused by addiction) on the part of the client; alternatively, it may simply reflect an honest difference of opinion about what is more important. One appropriate response to a client's persistent efforts to divert the agenda to discussions about relationship conflicts, work, or other family problems is an assurance that she or he will be referred to an appropriate resource following completion of this program, should those issues continue to be of concern at that time. In an extreme case, it may be necessary to make a referral so that the client can pursue his or her concern at the same time that he or she participates in this program. This would be the case, for example, if there was a clear risk of spousal or child abuse[2] or if the client appeared to be clinically depressed.

Reliance on Al-Anon or Nar-Anon

In this program, it is bonding with the fellowship of Al-Anon or Nar-Anon, and not the facilitator-client relationship, that is seen as being the major agent of change. The effective facilitator recognizes that active involvement in Al-Anon or Nar-Anon, including regular attendance at a variety of meetings, using the telephone to connect with other Al-Anon or Nar-Anon members on a regular basis, reading Al-Anon or Nar-Anon literature, and developing a relationship with a sponsor, is clearly preferable to increasing reliance on the facilitator. Similarly, the client should be encouraged to rely on the resources of Al-Anon or Nar-Anon, more so than on the facilitator, in times of crisis. Through these efforts, the facilitator plays a crucial role in helping to direct the client and get the process of change started.

Treatment Note: Responding to Crises

The facilitator's first response to a client's crisis, aside from sympathy and support, should be to encourage him or her to call an Al-Anon or Nar-Anon friend or sponsor or to go to a meeting as soon as possible. If the facilitator sees the need to schedule an emergency session to deal with a crisis, the goals for such a session should be the following:

To help the client assess the nature of the crisis in terms of how it threatens his or her personal well-being

To establish priorities: What can the client do immediately to deal with the problem in a way that is caring but consistent with detaching as opposed to enabling?

To clarify what resources within Al-Anon or Nar-Anon the client could turn to (calling another member, calling a sponsor, etc.) to support them at this time

Session Format

To allow the therapist to cover a fair amount of material in relatively few sessions, the format of therapy sessions is fairly structured in this program. Although the initial (assessment) session and the termination session of this program follow unique formats that are described in detail later, the practitioner should use the following format for all other sessions:

Part 1: Review

Beginning with Session 2, each session should start off with the facilitator checking in with the client, meaning a brief review (approximately 10 minutes) of the client's experiences since the last session, with special emphasis on Al-Anon or Nar-Anon meetings attended as well as on the client's efforts to detach in a constructive way from the addict. The latter includes efforts to stop enabling *plus* efforts on the part of the client to take care of his or her personal welfare independent of the addict. This opening portion of each session is crucial to establishing rapport and keeping the agenda of the program in focus. As much as possible, the facilitator should avoid protracted discussions of collateral issues (work, other family problems, children, etc.). The facilitator should keep the focus as much as possible on Al-Anon or Nar-Anon involvement, on the client's efforts to improve his or her own emotional and physical health, and on following up on any recovery tasks that were agreed to at the end of the last session. Concrete efforts to detach should be reinforced, and any "slips" the client may have had (into enabling) need to be discussed. In addition to the client's self-report, journal entries can be very helpful in facilitating the review process as well as in evaluating ongoing progress and establishing future recovery tasks.

Treatment Note: "Slips"

Within AA, a slip refers to a time when the alcoholic or addict drinks or uses drugs. AA traditionally approaches such episodes as serious but commonplace occurrences. Its stated goal is abstinence, but the fellowship by tradition recognizes that this is a long-term goal that is not typically achieved without setbacks. Even those with many years of sobriety may have occasional slips. What is most important at such times is that the addict or alcoholic be able to go to a meeting for support and disclose the slip. Slips are discussed in a nonjudgemental manner, with the emphasis being on what to do next (i.e., *how to avoid taking the next drink*). The addict who discloses a slip at a meeting can expect to have it acknowledged but without fear of recrimination. "We look for progress, not perfection" (AA, 1976, p. 60) is the response one is most likely to hear after disclosing a slip. Slips are thought of as times when the "powerful, baffling, and cunning" (AA, 1976, P. 58) illness of alcoholism or drug addiction has overcome the addict's best intentions to stay clean and sober. "Getting back on the wagon" is what is needed first and foremost at such times, and the group rightly recognizes and reinforces every hour of sobriety following a slip.

Within the context of Al-Anon and Nar-Anon, slips are occasions when a significant other enables the addict: either providing the means to drink or use or else helping the addict to avoid or minimize some negative consequence of drinking or using. A slip could also be thought of as a time when a significant other fails to maintain, in words and actions, an attitude of caring detachment toward the addict, for example by any of these actions:

Monitoring closely the addict's drinking or using

Attempting to hide or destroy liquor or drugs

Bargaining with the addict about how much they can drink or use

Giving "permission" to the addict to use or drink as a result of either nagging or pleading

Giving the addict money that the client knows very well will be used to support drinking or drugging

Covering up for the addict to an employer, friends, and so on

The goal of this intervention is to facilitate caring detachment and personal growth within the loved ones of substance abusers. To accomplish this, an open and honest relationship with the facilitator is critical. This includes being open about slips as described earlier. Through such open discussion, clients will develop a better understanding of caring detachment as well as tolerant attitudes toward themselves as they come to appreciate that detachment is a goal that is typically achieved incrementally. When discussing slips with clients, the therapeutic goal is to help them decide what to do next (i.e., the best thing to do *after* a slip that is consistent with Al-Anon or Nar-Anon philosophy).

Detaching, much like sobriety, is best thought of as a process that is characterized by progress that is punctuated by intermittent slips. Initially, significant others can be encouraged to detach in small ways—for instance, by letting the substance abuser know that they have chosen to seek help or that they have started going to Al-Anon or Nar-Anon meetings. Such simple acts break through the conspiracy of avoidance that is critical to enabling addiction to continue. As simple as they may sound, however, these acts often require real courage on the part of the significant other. They can elicit strong reactions in substance abusers for they herald the beginning of change in the addict-codependent relationship.

In addition to briefly reviewing any slips that may have occurred since the last session, some of the review time should be used to talk at least briefly about the client's reactions to readings and to any Al-Anon or Nar-Anon meetings that they attended since the last session. If no meetings were attended or if the client seems to be resisting going to meetings, the reasons for this resistance should be explored.

Part 2: New Material

Following the review, each session should move on to cover a specific focus: one of the eight core topics of the program as described in Part 2. It is very important that the facilitator help the client to understand all key concepts that are presented in these sessions, not only in an abstract intellectual sense but also concretely, in light of the client's experiences in relationship with the substance abuser. The goal, in other words, of presenting new material is to have it come alive for the client through discussions and examples that draw on the client's interactions with the substance abuser. The facilitator needs to be able to point to a specific incident and say "that is enabling," or "that is what is meant by detaching."

Part 3: Recovery Tasks

Each session ends with specific suggestions—recovery tasks—that clients are asked to follow through on between sessions. These are arrived at collaboratively with the client. Each topic covered in Part 2, however, includes many specific suggestions for relevant recovery tasks. Though brief, this last part of the session is very important and should be attended to with care, because recovery tasks are essentially grist for the mill for subsequent sessions.

The facilitator should attempt to assign recovery tasks in each of the following areas:

Meetings: A mutually agreed-on list of Al-Anon or Nar-Anon meetings to be attended by the client before the next session

Readings: Suggested readings that describe or illustrate 12-step recovery principles

Fellowship involvement: Suggested activities that will help to facilitate the client's active involvement and bonding with Al-Anon or Nar-Anon, such as making calls to Al-Anon or Nar-Anon members, approaching a potential sponsor, and so forth

Caring detachment: Suggestions for specific things the client can do to decrease his or her enabling of the substance abuser and increase caring detachment.

▨ Notes

1. The program presented in Part 2 was designed to be implemented in a total of 12 sessions over a period of up to 6 months. In a case management environment, practitioners may be pressed to work with an even more modest allocation of services. Under these circumstances, the issue of therapeutic focus becomes paramount.

2. Treatment of spousal or child abuse or neglect are not the subject of this book. Any professional planning to treat either substance abusers or their significant others, however, needs to be aware of the significant rates of concordance of abuse and addiction. Possible abuse should be explicitly ruled out or dealt with early in treatment. The clinician using the program described here may still proceed so long as any issues of abuse have been identified and triaged to appropriate treatment resources.

CHAPTER 3

On Giving Advice

THE ISSUE OF HOW BEST to deal with an addict or alcoholic that one is in a close relationship with is, of course, the focus of this program. Most if not all significant others will have made the decision to seek counseling at least in part not for themselves but to get concrete advice on how to get their loved ones to stop substance use, how to get them into treatment, or what to do when they get drunk or in trouble. These are all reasonable and common concerns. They are usually the results of chronic frustration and feelings of defeat. Not infrequently, a loved one will have tried, unsuccessfully, for years to accomplish these very goals.

In responding to clients, and particularly when asked for specific advice about what to do, the facilitator needs to be sure that whatever advice is given is consistent with 12-step fellowship traditions and philosophies. When offering advice, it is important to keep in mind that AA, Al-Anon, and other 12-step fellowships are remarkably pluralistic and nondogmatic. They have a spiritual core, and they possess a fund of wisdom about addiction and recovery. However, aside from their singular emphasis on abstinence as the goal of recovery, they are remarkably flexible: spiritually pluralistic and decidedly pragmatic about how to stay sober one day at a time. They implicitly recognize that the number of useful strategies for staying sober (or its equivalent in significant others, which is maintaining caring detachment in word and deed) are as varied as the number of people who make up the fellowships. The bottom line is what works for the individual addict or his or her loved one, meaning how she or he has succeeded in staying sober or detaching. Although it is true that 12-step fellowships use slogans heavily, these reflect broad statements of philosophy, not specific advice. Therapists should adopt a similarly flexible and pragmatic approach when offering advice.

Al-Anon and Nar-Anon traditions suggest that it is best to approach the issue of advice giving in a collaborative way—as something that is flexible and, therefore, open to discussion—as opposed to presenting it in any way as dogma handed down by the therapist. The subtitle of a popular AA publication, *Living Sober* (AA, 1975), for example, is simply this: "Some methods that AA members have used for not drinking." Similarly, recovery tasks and suggestions about detachment strategies are best approached as practical *suggestions,* which clients are free to modify to suit their particular situations and their relationships to the substance abusers. For example, strategies that would make sense for a spouse to use might have to be modified for a parent, sibling, or adult child of a substance abuser.

The facilitator should also be aware that what works for one significant other may be precisely the wrong thing for another. Consider the following example: One partner of an alcoholic man was accustomed to confronting him and complaining often about his drinking. Over a period of years, this dynamic had come to represent the status quo of the relationship. The alcoholic had grown accustomed to it. He knew that at least once a week, he and his wife would argue about his drinking. But he also knew that that would be the end of it. The storm would pass and the next day everything would be back to "normal" in the house. In an ironic way, the fighting served to enable his drinking, because it was a sign that nothing in the relationship had changed. So they kept on fighting, and he kept on drinking.

For another spouse, the situation was exactly the opposite. This relationship had evolved into a conspiracy of silence about drinking. The wife never mentioned it, although both spouses knew she was concerned about it. She just avoided her husband when he was drunk, and she never brought the issue up when he was sober. In this case, it was silence, not fighting, that represented the enabling response. Silence between this couple represented the relational status quo. So long as the wife was silent, the husband, like the one in the first example, could feel secure that nothing had really changed and he could go on drinking as usual.

In guiding each of these wives toward caring detachment, the same facilitator offered them exactly the opposite advice. To the first, she advised *not* fighting. Instead, she suggested leaving the house to spend time with other family or friends or going to an Al-Anon meeting whenever her husband got drunk. In contrast, she advised the second wife to start to comment to her husband—when he was *sober*—on how much he drank and how much money he spent every week on liquor. The facilitator cautioned this wife not to get into a shouting match with her husband when he was drinking, or to debate whether or not he was an alcoholic. She was told to simply remark about the amount, the frequency, and the cost.

These examples on giving advice illustrate the fact that concepts such as enabling and detaching reflect *dynamic processes* within the addict-codependent relationship. Contrary to what some therapists may expect, there are few hard and fast rules as to what behaviors constitute enabling and which constitute detaching. Obviously, stopping at a liquor store every day on the way home from work and buying your alcoholic spouse a fifth of vodka would constitute enabling, period. And allowing a substance abuser to experience the negative consequences of drinking or drug use would certainly constitute detaching. Many other situations, however, are less clear. Determining what is enabling and what is caring detachment depends in part on understanding the dynamics of the relationship and then deciding what behavior would represent a change in the status quo—in other words, what would help the codependent break old and ineffective patterns of relating and thereby send a message to the addict that something has changed. In both of the examples given, the alcoholics had clear and immediate reactions to the change in their wives' behavior—to the change in the dynamics of their *relationships.* Moreover, both wives reported that the new ways of relating made them feel better about themselves.

Al-Anon and Nar-Anon, as fellowships of individuals who are in relationships with addicts, have strong traditions of providing unqualified support as well as a wealth of practical advice to all who wish to avail themselves of it. Al-Anon and Nar-Anon are widespread, and their resources are readily available. The facilitator should attempt to steer the client consistently toward Al-Anon or Nar-Anon as *the* primary source of support and advice about what to do about his or her relationship with the addict. The resources that Al-Anon and Nar-Anon have to offer include meetings, telephone networks and hot lines, sponsors, and literature.

As another example of a situation that might arise, consider this scenario: A woman has her therapist paged in the middle of the night. She is extremely distressed. Her husband, she says, was just arrested for the second time for driving while intoxicated and is in the local lockup. She is worried that her husband will miss more days at work, where he has already been in trouble for excessive absences. She also fears that he may be subject to dismissal if it's discovered that he has been arrested. On the other hand, she realizes that this arrest is just another in a long string of negative consequences that are the result of her husband's alcoholism. Part of her wants to detach: to let him face the consequences, rather than mitigating those consequences by going to the lockup and bonding him out. However, she is conflicted over how to respond to her husband's emphatic demand that she drive there and post bond immediately. In a phone conversation with her, he was alternately tearful, angry, and pleading, saying that he "can't stand being locked up like an animal."

The therapist may understandably feel pressed to give an immediate response to this woman. Indeed, some therapeutic response is called for. However, this can be done in one of two ways. First, the therapist could help the client work through her ambivalence and reach a decision, right there over the phone. Given the demands of the woman's husband, both the client and the therapist could feel pressured to work the issue through and reach a decision immediately. However, another approach would be to ask the client if she had considered calling an Al-Anon friend, or her sponsor if she has one, or even deferring a decision until she could get to a meeting and talk it out. The facilitator in this situation could reinforce the idea that no matter what the client decides to do, she should recognize how difficult her position is, and how painful it can be to detach. The therapist can validate that it is appropriate for the client to take some time to think and to take advantage of Al-Anon as a place to vent her thoughts and feelings and to seek comfort and support. The facilitator can point out sympathetically that this very situation has no doubt been faced by many others and that knowing what others had done and seeking their counsel and support can be a great stress reliever.

Should the facilitator decide to help this client reach a decision, then the facilitator should be guided by the general principle of helping the codependent identify alternative courses of action, decide which would be enabling and which would be detaching, and encourage the detached response as being the better one in the long run. In this example, a first step might be to ask the wife what she would usually do in that situation and what would be the likely consequences of that course of action on her husband's drinking in the long run. Another way to put it is this: "If you were to bail your husband out tonight, would that motivate him to think about not drinking or would it help maintain the status quo?"

Al-Anon and Nar-Anon clearly advocate caring detachment and favor allowing the drinker or user to experience the natural consequences of substance use. In this example, that would mean not bailing the alcoholic husband out, at least not immediately. His wife may need a great deal of emotional support for that decision. The therapist must be able to sympathize with the anxieties that detaching creates and support the courage that it takes to break free from enabling. This is no mean task and requires at times a virtual leap of faith—a belief in the ultimate wisdom of "tough love." This is what is meant by *surrender* within the Al-Anon and Nar-Anon fellowships. It is also why Al-Anon and Nar-Anon are so important, for they will continue to be there for the client long after treatment has been terminated.

Should the client give in to her anxieties and bail her husband out, the therapist must be careful not to judge her harshly for that decision. Rather, the therapist should recognize that detaching is hard work and suggest that perhaps the client can begin detaching in less stressful situations. Detaching is a process that can be shaped, beginning with small actions and leading to bolder ones. One useful approach to this is to help the significant other develop a *detaching hierarchy* that starts by identifying little ways to detach and then identifies progressively bolder steps toward caring detachment. In this example, not bailing the husband out would clearly fall on the "bolder detaching" side of the hierarchy.

The same resources that are available to the client are also available to the facilitator. Specifically, Chapter 8 ("To Wives") in *Alcoholics Anonymous* (AA, 1976), the stories in *Al-Anon Faces Alcoholism* (Al-Anon, 1985), and Al-Anon and Nar-Anon meetings are all places that the facilitator can turn to for guidance in giving advice to clients. Practitioners who are aware of and avail themselves of these materials and resources may have an advantage in counseling clients when it comes to making difficult decisions.

CHAPTER 4

Motivating the Substance Abuser to Change

VIRTUALLY ALL SIGNIFICANT OTHERS of substance abusers would like a concrete answer to the question that nags them: What can I do to get my loved one to give up alcohol or drugs? It has already been suggested here that detaching promotes reevaluation and change in the addict-codependent relationship, whereas enabling undermines any motivation for such reevaluation or change. Paradoxically, Al-Anon and Nar-Anon initiate the change process by asking loved ones to admit that they are powerless by themselves to change the addicts' behavior. This is Step 1: *We admitted that we were powerless over alcohol—that our lives had become unmanageable.*

Another way of framing this to a client is to suggest that the current dynamics of his or her relationship with the addict effectively promotes the status quo instead of promoting change. In other words, "The way you've been relating to the substance abuser hasn't promoted significant or lasting change, so why not put that aside for awhile and try a different approach?"

Behaviorally oriented family therapies for substance abuse also recognize that problems such as substance abuse can be influenced by social consequences within the family. They attempt to modify it through behavioral interventions, most often enlisting the spouse as the agent of change (McCrady & Epstein, 1996). Some such approaches to intervention with concerned significant others, most notably the Community Reinforcement Approach (CRA; Meyers & Smith, 1995; Meyers, Dominguez, & Smith, 1996) advocate shaping the substance abuser's drinking or drug use through the direct application of reward, extinction, or response incompatibility strategies by the loved one. For example, the wife of an alcoholic may be encouraged to praise her husband whenever he does not drink and also to offer other reinforcements, such as physical affection or small gifts. In contrast, she may be encouraged to show no response at all to continued using or drinking (i.e., extinction). And she may be encouraged to engage her husband in activities (e.g., going to a movie) that are incompatible with drinking. CRA advises loved ones to avoid excessive arguing with the substance abuser in the belief that punishment is not as effective as reward and extinction in altering behavior.

The goals of behaviorally oriented interventions, such as CRA, and this 12-step-oriented intervention overlap to the extent that both see motivating a substance abuser to change as desirable. However, there are significant differences. CRA clearly seeks to use loved ones as primary agents of change through teaching them behavior modification techniques. The goal of treatment is primarily on motivating the substance abuser to drink or use less, with the overall mental health of the significant other being more or less secondary. In contrast, in Al-Anon and Nar-Anon, as in this program, the emphasis is reversed, with more importance placed on the recovery and growth of the loved one. Getting the substance abuser to stop or decrease use or get into treatment is desirable but is also seen as being more likely as the loved ones' emotional, spiritual, and physical health improve and as they change the way they relate to the addict in a fundamental way.

The 12-step approach to motivating the substance abuser to change, then, differs from behavioral approaches, such as CRA, in philosophy and approach. The concept of caring detachment emphasizes allowing the substance abuser to experience the natural consequences of his or her problem, as opposed to shielding him or her in any way, and asks significant others to place responsibility for recovery on the substance abusers while focusing on their own emotional, social, and spiritual needs. This is not to say that the concerned other rejects, attacks, or rebukes the substance abuser. However, the end result of successful detachment is a vastly different addict-codependent relationship and a much healthier codependent. As one mother of two adult alcoholic sons put it,

> I realized it was time for me to let them go and for me to take care of me. Even if they died—and this is really difficult for me to say—I knew that I would go on. I had done my best—I had loved them—and now I had to let them go. (Dick Young Productions, 1988)

Al-Anon describes caring detachment in the following way:

> For Al-Anon members, detachment is the culmination of applying themselves to all the steps and slogans of the Al-Anon program, especially the first step. This necessitates accepting a concept of powerlessness over another human being and over alcoholism. In order to reach the kind of detachment that

Al-Anon members strive for, the individual must come to understand and accept his or her own feelings, attitudes, prejudices, and actions and be committed to changing them in a healthy way. (Al-Anon, 1985, p. 29)

Clearly, the foregoing passage suggests that the process of detaching from the substance abuser goes beyond merely allowing him or her to suffer the natural consequences of the problem, unmitigated by concerned others. Such behaviors may be signs of detachment, but detachment itself appears to be a process of significant internal change or growth as well, including developing the capacity for humility and acceptance. These same sentiments are expressed in the following words of a woman who was the wife of an alcoholic and the mother of four chemically dependent sons:

Learning to detach is a great kindness to ourselves and to the chemically dependent person, and well worth overcoming the obstacles in the beginning. One reward of detachment is that it frees us to grow, to "live and let live." (Carolyn W., 1984, pp. 7-8)

The foregoing quote recognizes that the goal of detachment is not achieved easily and requires substantial internal changes in attitudes and beliefs to support its outward behavioral manifestations. Indeed, sustained detachment could be said to be the result of a profound change in a person's outlook on life and on relationships in general. This seems to be the case for those whom this writer has known well and who have impressed him as models of caring detachment. Carolyn W. (1984) offers the following advice for those who wish to pursue this goal:

In the process of rebuilding our relationship, I've found several things that help in my emotional and mental stability, and help guide me through detachment:

1. The absence of suspicion and resentment. Nursing a grudge was a major factor in my unhappiness.

2. Not living in the past. An unwholesome preoccupation with old mistakes and failures leads to depression.

3. Not wasting time and energy fighting conditions I cannot change. I cooperate with life instead of trying to run away from it.

4. I force myself to stay involved with others. I resist the temptation to withdraw and become reclusive during periods of emotional stress.

5. I refuse to indulge in self-pity when life hands me a raw deal.

6. I cultivate the old-fashioned virtues—love, honor, compassion, loyalty. (p. 16)

Two things stand out in Carolyn W.'s list. The first is that detachment as a *pattern of behavior* (e.g., not bonding out a partner who has been arrested for the second time for driving while intoxicated) is correlated with detachment as a *set of values* and an approach to relationships and to life in general. Although we will be asking significant others to identify and try out behaviors consistent with detaching, the facilitator should recognize that there is a level deeper than this—a constellation of character traits that underlie and support these new ways of relating to the substance abuser and indeed, to one's self. The process of character growth and spiritual renewal that leads to this result is best achieved when the individual bonds to a 12-step fellowship and begins to incorporate the 12-step program in his or her day-to-day life. The 12th step of AA explicitly recognizes the profound nature of this change when it talks about spiritual awakening: "Having had a spiritual awakening as the result of these steps, we tried to carry this message to alcoholics, and to practice these principles in all our affairs" (AA, 1976, p. 60).

This step applies to Al-Anon as well. Often associated in peoples' minds only with becoming a sponsor and "spreading the word" of recovery, the 12th step actually emphasizes the need to live a life consistent with the steps, most of which have more to do with character development than addiction. This may well explain why a single family member's recovery can, in the long run, affect an entire family so profoundly.

Also noteworthy in the earlier quote is that there is no inherent incompatibility between detaching and loyalty: One can be loyal yet still detach. In fact, detaching may be more loving than enabling. Recently, this has been called *tough love*. This is an important point to keep in mind because substance abusers often accuse their loved ones of disloyalty when they first begin to detach.

* * *

The preceding discussion of detachment is relevant in several ways to the issue of motivating the substance abuser to change. It is important because although substance abuse and addiction is a problem of the individual, it also has a relational component. As we shall see later, addiction itself can be framed in relational terms. In addition, relational patterns between the addict and the codependent can either support the addictive process (enabling) or undermine it (detaching). As the following two examples illustrate, enabling refers to those attitudes and behaviors in the codependent that support the status quo in the relationship, thereby also supporting the addictive process. Conversely, detaching upsets the relational status quo. Time and time again, we have seen how successful detaching affects not only the codependent but the substance abuser as well. The facilitator should keep this fact in mind because loved ones not infrequently become anxious when it is suggested that they "let go" of the substance abuser. If uninformed about the true nature and dynamics of detaching, they may mistake such advice for rejecting or giving up on the substance abuser, indeed on the relationship itself. It will be important to assure clients that changing the way they relate to the substance abuser will prove, in the long run, to be the most effective way to motivate him or her to change and is, in truth, an act of caring.

Margaret sought out treatment for herself because she felt depressed and hopeless about her situation. She was 60 years old, a successful administrator in a state agency. Normally, she would have been looking forward to a comfortable retirement, but unfortunately, her situation was anything but normal. She had three grown sons, ranging in age from 26 to 34, all of whom lived with her and all of whom were alcoholics. The oldest had been unemployed since losing his driver's license 6 months earlier, following a third DWI (driving while intoxicated) arrest. He was also divorced, and when he had his 5-year-old daughter on alternate weekends, he pretty much handed her over to Margaret.

Widowed when her youngest son was 3 years old, Margaret had supported all of her sons by herself. Their father had also been an alcoholic, though he had managed to work steadily and was not abusive. She described him as "a quiet drunk—basically a sweet man, but with little confidence, who loved me in his way." As a single mother and the sole parent, she tended to be somewhat indulgent of her sons. "I've never liked saying no to them," she explained. "For a long time, whenever I'd say no, I'd feel guilty—like I had traumatized them. It took me awhile to realize that they were just 'normally' frustrated and angry."

Margaret was almost as indulgent now as she had been when her sons were boys. When she started treatment, she was doing virtually all the cooking and cleaning in the house and paid all the major household expenses. Her sons spent their earnings mostly on cars, clothes, and booze. The longest any one of them had lived away from home was 6 months, when the youngest one did a semester at college before dropping out.

It was understandable why Margaret saw her situation as hopeless. There seemed no end in sight to her sons' dependency—on her and on alcohol. The few times she had broached the subjects of moving out or of doing something about drinking with any of them, she'd been rebuffed. Although she recognized her own depression, what she needed most of all, she said, was some guidance in changing her situation. Someone had told her about Al-Anon and the idea of letting go of her sons, but she had not yet been to a meeting, and she had no idea of what "letting go" meant. Despite her frustrations, she still loved her sons. Moreover, on some level, she still felt guilty and responsible for their addictions. In her words, "I want to help them, not reject them." To her way of thinking, her friend's advice smacked of rejection.

In Margaret's case, it did indeed take some doing for her to see the difference between caring detachment and rejection. As it turned out, this was due in part to the fact that she did harbor resentments toward her sons—resentments that she had been reluctant to admit. Secretly, she feared that once she allowed herself to express anger, she might explode with rage. When she was able to accept these feelings and find a sympathetic ear in her therapist, she was able to work them through to the extent that she no longer feared that detaching would turn into cruel rejection. She started going to Al-Anon meetings. The first two she went to didn't appeal to her, but her counselor continued to encourage her. They both networked among friends and finally found two meetings that Margaret felt quite comfortable in. Within a month, she had a sponsor whom she spoke with over the phone several times a week and often met for coffee on Sunday mornings.

Margaret started to detach in small ways. This is the approach advocated because it is typically less threatening and leads to initial successes that help to boost the codependent's self-confidence. Margaret began by making a point of meeting friends for dinner, or eating at their houses, two or three times a week, leaving her sons to fend for themselves when it came to dinner. She also started sorting the laundry piles, doing her own and leaving her sons' for them. The response was immediate. "They're all complaining," she said to her therapist with a laugh, "that there's no food in the house and that they have no clothes to wear!" Margaret responded to these complaints in the way she and her therapist had decided: She told her sons that she thought it was neither in her interest nor theirs to continue to do all the cooking or cleaning. That was treating them like children, she explained, when they were obviously grown men. Grudgingly, they started making their own arrangements for meals several times a week. Margaret noticed that they complained, but they did not starve.

Next, Margaret asked her sons to start contributing $50 a week each toward the household expenses—heat, electricity, and so on. They complained again, all three saying that they couldn't afford it. Her unemployed son accused her of "kicking him when he was down." But Margaret stuck to her guns. She knew very well that her sons seemed able enough to come up with drinking money, but until now, she'd never said anything about it. Now she said this:

> We all have expenses, and we all have to decide how we're going to spend our money. I've been thinking about selling this house anyway, because it's becoming too expensive to maintain on my income alone. I have to start planning for retirement. I've been thinking about doing that in 2 years. At that point, I plan to sell the place and buy a condominium. But if you men can't help support it until then, I may have to sell it sooner.

Again, the men complained, but somehow they each came up with their $50. Her unemployed son found a job, and one of the others drove him there and back every day. Margaret also noticed that they were using the washer and dryer more often and that the refrigerator had some food in it.

The last thing that Margaret did was to leave the materials she'd been reading—about alcoholism—in the living room where they could be seen by all. Up until then, she'd kept them in her bedroom, where she read them at night after going to bed. Now, she left them on the coffee table and read them in the living room. Her sons seemed tense whenever she would pick up one of these books. Finally, the oldest one broke the ice and asked, "Why are you reading that stuff, Mom? You're not an alcoholic." Margaret had her answer ready. She said,

> Because your father was, and because all three of you boys have drinking problems, too, in my opinion. I want to understand it better. I've also been seeing someone to get some help in understanding how I can separate myself from your problems and start taking care of myself a little.

After an awkward moment of silence, her son replied that he felt that Margaret had been rejecting him and his brothers lately and questioned whether she was being "brainwashed by a shrink." Margaret said that she was making her own decisions.

> I'm simply learning to let you boys be responsible for yourselves. Of course, I think *you* boys ought to see someone about your drinking or else go to AA. But that's your decision to make. I'm doing this for me.

As the months rolled by, Margaret's self-esteem grew steadily. She started saving the money her sons gave her, continued going to Al-Anon meetings, and proceeded with her plans for retirement. She made a point of not keeping this secret, to the extent that she had a realtor come and give her an estimate of how much she could expect to sell the house for, as well as a retirement counselor who came and spoke with her about managing her income and expenses after retiring.

It was just over a year after Margaret began therapy and started going to Al-Anon that one son—the middle one—signed himself into an alcohol rehabilitation program. Two months later, her oldest son told her he'd started going to AA meetings with his brother. Soon after that, the youngest son—still drinking—moved out of the house. In assessing the way things had gone, Margaret had this to say: "I would never have imagined that things could change so much in my family just by me changing myself."

Ron's case was somewhat less dramatic than Margaret's, but it is just as illustrative of how detaching works. He had been married to Joan for 25 years. He'd retired from the military 2 years earlier, and that was when what had been mere suspicion for several years became obvious: His wife had a drinking problem. He'd brought the issue up once or twice, but each time, she had reacted with anger. Being a man who disliked intense conflict in his personal relationships, he dropped the subject rather than risking a blow-up.

Ron explained that Joan started drinking wine every day at about 3:00 or 4:00 in the afternoon. By dinnertime, she had pretty much finished off a bottle. Despite this, Ron described their life together as generally good. They were pretty active and healthy and had a lot of friends whom they socialized with. Aside from Joan's tendency to be irritable on occasion, the only major complaint he had was that she would usually fall asleep on the couch by 9:00 at night. Before he'd retired, Ron thought this was just because she was tired; but now, he knew the truth, and he admitted it bothered him. "It gets kind of lonely and boring being up by yourself every night," he said. "And knowing that it's due to her drinking makes it all the more annoying."

Joan tried to rationalize her problem away by saying it was "just wine" she was drinking. "I don't touch hard liquor and you know it!" she shot back once when Ron very tentatively brought up the issue of drinking. He had gone to a few Al-Anon meetings, and he recognized this response as denial at work. He'd heard stories about how inventive alcoholics could be when it came to finding excuses to drink and also how defensive they could be when it came to minimizing the extent that alcohol was affecting their lives.

Ron's detachment came in a very simple but ultimately very effective form. It seemed that he too enjoyed wine but only with dinner, and he drank moderately—rarely more than two glasses a night and usually only one. He still enjoyed it, but he confessed that ever since he realized that Joan was getting drunk almost every day, his pleasure had diminished considerably. Naturally, Joan encouraged his drinking, because it provided a convenient cover for her own. She would even suggest that they go shopping together to look for good wine values.

Eventually, Ron came to appreciate how his own wine drinking constituted a signal to Joan: "Everything's OK, go ahead and drink." Once he realized the role that he was unwittingly playing in his wife's substance abuse problem, he became even more uncomfortable with their nightly dinner rituals. He finally decided that he would stop. He told Joan that he was not happy with himself about drinking every day and wanted to change his pattern. He'd drink, he said, occasionally, over a meal, but had decided to largely forego it as a daily event. She could drink if she chose to, he said, but most of the time he would not.

Predictably, Joan reacted strongly. She accused Ron of "moralizing" about drinking, and she said he was giving up drinking in an attempt to "control" her. Ron was ready for this. He replied that Joan was an adult and reiterated that she was free to make her own decisions about drinking. But he was also adult and was making his own decision.

For the next several weeks, Ron reported to his counselor, he and Joan fought more than they had in their whole marriage, not necessarily over drinking but over little things. At the same time, he noticed that Joan drank less in the afternoon. And although she continued to drink wine with dinner even when he did not, she drank less then, too. This new pattern continued for several months. Ron was resistant to going back to Al-Anon, but he stuck by his decision to change his own behavior; in fact, his own drinking decreased even more over time. Meanwhile, he increased his exercising and, overall, felt much healthier.

* * *

The cases described illustrate how detaching affects both the codependent and the substance abuser. Detaching does involve allowing a substance abuser to experience the natural consequences of his or her problem, but clearly, effective detaching also goes well beyond this. In Part 2 of this book, the reader will be given more specific direction in facilitating caring detachment. It is a process that encompasses both behaviors and attitudes, and it can become a powerful force for change in the addict-codependent relationship.

CHAPTER 5

Recovery and the Process of Group Bonding

ACTIVELY FACILITATING a significant other's involvement in a 12-step fellowship is a powerful way to help that person deal with the impact that addiction or substance abuse has had on him or her and the family. Secondarily, involvement in Al-Anon or Nar-Anon, and specifically learning to develop a relationship with the substance abuser that is based on caring detachment as opposed to enabling, can be a potent means of motivating a substance abuser to change. Over the long run, the most appropriate and effective agent of change for the loved ones of addicts is to be found in group involvement as opposed to the therapeutic relationship, which, in this era of managed care, is becoming increasingly temporal.

To achieve these goals, the facilitator needs to understand the process by which an individual goes from being a nonmember of a mutual-help group to an individual who could be said to be bonded to it and committed to following its program in day-to-day life. That process, of course, begins with attending meetings.

▒ Attendance

Bonding begins with being there. It is helpful for the therapist to be familiar with the format of the group that a client is being referred to so that the client can be prepared. Knowing in advance what to expect when one first walks into an Al-Anon or Nar-Anon meeting can help to place the client at ease and facilitate his or her introduction to a mutual-help fellowship. Clients who are prone to social anxiety, who express exceptional guilt and shame in connection with their loved ones' substance abuse problems, or who worry about potential exposure may hesitate to take even the first step toward using a mutual-help group, which, of course, is to get to a meeting.

Al-Anon, Nar-Anon, and other 12-step meetings can vary considerably in format. So-called *open meetings* are open to persons who do not necessarily have a loved one with an alcohol or drug problem, whereas *closed meetings* are to be attended only by men and women who acknowledge being in such relationships. Meetings last from an hour to an hour and a half. Time is set aside for socializing and networking (e.g., getting phone numbers, approaching potential sponsors) either before or after the formal meeting. Each meeting has a chairperson who is elected by the group and, usually, a secretary. These offices and responsibilities typically change hands periodically.

Descriptions of some of the different types of 12-step meetings follow:

Speaker Meeting

At these meetings, which are highly recommended for newcomers, members of the group as well as occasional "guest speakers" relate the stories of their experiences with addiction and recovery. The format of these stories is as follows: how things were, what happened, how things are now. This is the core story of addiction and recovery, and it is ultimately the basis for bonding. Occasionally, an Al-Anon group will invite a recovering alcoholic or addict to tell his or her story of addiction and recovery.

Discussion Meeting

The format here is to select a topic (e.g., gratitude, shame, grief, detachment, enabling, resentments) and to share one's thoughts about it. Typically, either the chairperson selects the topic or the members do so in rotation. Sometimes, the topic is a reading from *Al-Anon Faces Alcoholism* (Al-Anon, 1985), *One Day At a Time In Al-Anon* (Al-Anon, 1986), or another AA, Al-Anon, Nar-Anon, or NA publication. Even simple listening at discussion meetings can help to instill renewed hope in a newcomer, help him or her to see the relationship with the substance abuser from a new perspective, and desensitize the shame and guilt that are associated with addiction.

Step Meeting

In step meetings, the format is to read one of the 12 steps and then for members to share their thoughts about how they as individuals are "working" that step, how they are attempting to implement it in their day-to-day lives and particularly in their relationships with the substance abusers. Newcomers have an opportunity at step meetings to learn how others have interpreted the steps and how they relate to the lifestyle and attitude changes that are associated with caring detachment and recovery. Some step meetings limit themselves to the first three steps, whereas others include all 12 steps as topics for reflection and discussion.

Treatment Note: Reassuring the Nervous Newcomer

It is said within 12-step fellowships that "the most important person in a meeting is the newcomer." Virtually all 12-step meetings take pains to greet newcomers and to make them feel welcome. Al-Anon (1986), for example, has this say:

> The newcomer to Al-Anon usually feels alone in a hostile world, drowning in a sea of troubles. To be sure, some may have been of her [sic] own making, but all of us had much to learn about living with an alcoholic before we could begin to create a serene and orderly world within us. Let us not be too eager to swamp this confused person with advice. A warm welcome and words of hope and reassurance will be all the therapy she can use at first. One member, too, should offer a protecting wing and a willing ear to her troubles, if she cares to talk about them after the meeting. (p. 206)

The facilitator should be aware of this tradition of welcoming and not pressuring newcomers. It stems from an even more fundamental 12-step tradition: that it should be *attraction,* and opposed to *promotion,* that draws individuals to the fellowship (AA, 1952). The newcomer can therefore be assured that she or he will not be unduly pressured to sign up or commit. Those unfamiliar with 12-step fellowships commonly harbor such expectations, and they can be one reason why a client may be reluctant to give Al-Anon or Nar-Anon a try. It is often helpful to ask the client to share whatever fears or negative expectations they may have and then to share the information just given about what they can more likely expect when they go to a meeting.

Those being referred to meetings for the first time are helped if the therapist can provide them with a current meeting schedule. If the therapist cannot get a schedule, information about meetings is usually available through a public information service line, which is listed in local telephone books. Published schedules list the times and places of all meetings and also indicate what type of meetings they are and whether there are any restrictions (e.g., nonsmoking, women only).

In addition to the generic types of meetings, there are also a growing number of specialty meetings: men's meetings, women's meetings, meetings for seniors, meetings for parents, and so forth. The formats of all meetings tend to be informal: Members can elect to speak or simply to listen, and they can leave whenever they choose to.

Whatever particular group the facilitator is attempting to use as part of treatment, educating the significant other about what to expect can facilitate initial involvement. Also, specific therapeutic interventions, such as simple encouragement, making specific suggestions ("Just go and listen the first few times"), problem solving (e.g., transportation or child care issues), and even role-playing ("Let's practice how you can introduce yourself") can all be brought to bear toward the end of helping the client get started with a 12-step group.

Identification

The process of bonding is facilitated when the newcomer is able to identify with other members of the group. The telling of personal stories is a strong tradition within 12-step fellowships and forms the basis for identification. Listening to stories of addiction and recovery—how it was; what happened; how it is now—is a concrete means through which newcomers can feel connected to others. The ability to experience commonality in this way bridges differences in sex, ethnicity, and other factors that might otherwise undermine the bonding process. It helps to define the commonalities that bring people together, despite their many other differences. These commonalities include not only typical relationship issues, such as conflicts with the substance abuser over money or responsibilities, but also intrapsychic issues, such as dealing with anxiety over what will happen to the family if the codependent begins to detach and guilt associated with fears that the codependent may have that they somehow caused the problem.

"Identify, don't compare," is the advice often given to the AA newcomer. The same would be true for the newcomer to Al-Anon or Nar-Anon. The facilitator can expect to encounter more or less resistance to this idea of identifying with others, and the more that resistance can be worked through, the more the client can be expected to begin to bond with the group.

Most often, resistance at this stage takes the form of the client drawing contrasts between himself or herself and others in the group as opposed to focusing on commonalities. These contrasts may be based on age, sex, education, occupational class, religiosity, income, and even interests. The motivation behind drawing such contrasts quickly becomes apparent: The anxious or uncomfortable client is emphasizing differences to resist identifying with the group and justify rejecting it. She or he is avoiding the bonding process. For the addict, this bonding occurs when the newcomer to AA or NA identifies with the core story of Alcoholics Anonymous, which is a story of a journey from powerlessness and hopelessness to empowerment and renewal through commitment to "a new community of interpretation and action" (Fowler, 1993, pp. 115-116). So it is for the significant other. A comparable theme—of a journey from despair to renewal—applies to the journey that the loved ones of substance abusers face. The resistant alcoholic or addict rejects the notion of powerlessness and clings instead to an illusion that personal willpower alone will succeed in controlling substance use. Similarly, codependents often resist the idea that their love and willpower is not enough to overcome the substance abuse problems. Of course, by clinging to this idea, most codependents unwittingly enable the problem to continue.

Many addicts as well as many significant others initially balk at the mere mention of the word "powerlessness." It has been pointed out, however, that there is "a kind of power that issues from acknowledged powerlessness" (Fowler, 1993, p. 116). That power has its roots in collective identification and bonding: in the strength that comes from having the humility to accept personal limitation and the faith that comes from a willingness to trust others and follow the collective wisdom of those who have made the same journey that one is now facing. To the extent that the facilitator can help the resistant client identify with key elements of other members' stories, she or he also helps indirectly to empower that client.

Networking

Networking is an integral part of all 12-step fellowships. All groups strongly encourage members to build a support network by establishing contact with other members on a regular basis. AA calls this *telephone therapy* (AA, 1975). It is equally encouraged in Al-Anon and Nar-Anon. The facilitator should consequently also take pains to encourage significant others to network. The therapist can describe its purpose as establishing a safety net in advance of the need for one: of having a network of friends already in place *before* problems occur.

Building a network can also be critical as the client begins to detach from the addict. Through telephone therapy and personal contact before or after meetings, the newcomer begins to make new friends and establish himself or herself in a new peer group—one that is moving away from codependence toward a healthier way of relating to the substance abusers.

Sponsorship

Sponsorship is unique to 12-step fellowships. It had its origins in recovering alcoholics who were willing to assume responsibility for other detoxified alcoholics when they were discharged from hospitals (Kurtz, 1988). From those beginnings, the role of the sponsor evolved into that of guide and mentor. The relationship of the "sponsee" to the sponsor is an important one but especially so for the newcomer. An effective sponsor is an invaluable asset to the newcomer. Without a sponsor as a resource, the client is apt to turn to the facilitator for advice and support when that advice and support could be obtained through the Al-Anon or Nar-Anon fellowships. The facilitator should therefore consistently encourage and, if necessary, coach the client regarding how to find and use an initial (temporary) Al-Anon or Nar-Anon sponsor.

The sponsor should be someone of the same sex as the client. A sponsor should also be someone who is active in the fellowship and who has established some clear detachment from the alcoholic or addict in his or her life. Last, the sponsor should be someone who possesses what the client perceives to be a good, indeed even admirable, character and who leads a healthy lifestyle that the client would like to emulate in at least some ways.

In monitoring whether the newcomer-sponsor relationship is working well, the facilitator should inquire as to how often the newcomer speaks to the sponsor (hopefully, often) and whether the sponsor is making specific suggestions about meetings, detaching, and so on. A sponsor is *not* a therapist, however, and a good sponsor will limit the relationship to what they know best, which is how to use the resources of Al-Anon and Nar-Anon and how to work the 12-step program one day at a time. Developing a relationship with a sponsor constitutes an important step toward bonding with the fellowship.

Rituals and Traditions

Participation in rituals and traditions have always represented a vehicle whereby the individual bonds to any group. Twelve-step fellowships, including Al-Anon and Nar-Anon, are rich with rituals and traditions that bond members together. The newcomer who is ambivalent about the group can be expected to be uncomfortable with rituals and therefore reticent to participate in them wholeheartedly. Typical rituals include reciting the "Serenity Prayer" as a group, acknowledging and celebrating members' anniversaries of active membership, storytelling, and so on.

Other traditions that newcomers can partake of include what is called service work: setting up chairs, making coffee, and cleanup after meetings. These simple contributions to the group can help to bond the newcomer to it over time and should be encouraged. Newcomers who are socially shy and inclined to be quiet listeners at meetings can begin to bond through volunteering for service work.

Because AA and its sister 12-step fellowships are intentionally decentralized, many individual groups develop their own unique rituals and traditions. The therapist is likely to learn of these from the newcomer who reports back on his or her latest experiences with the group. By understanding the important role that these rituals and traditions play in cementing the relationship to the group and encouraging the newcomer to give it a try and keep an open mind, the facilitator can play a significant role in transferring the locus of therapeutic change from the client-therapist relationship to the client-group relationship.

* * *

The foregoing has been a brief look at the process by which a newcomer to Al-Anon or Nar-Anon can be helped to bond to those fellowships. This is not a passive process, and the more active the therapist can be in promoting it, the more likely it is that his or her client will make the connections necessary to support the process of detachment.

CHAPTER 6

Getting What You Wish For

Family Issues in Early Recovery

THERE IS AN OLD SAYING that goes something like this: "Be careful what you wish for, for you just might get it." Perhaps this is intended as a warning to the chronically malcontent; or perhaps it is a message about appreciating what we have. In either case, there is a kernel of wisdom here, in that change—even change we deeply wish for—can produce results that we may not anticipate or necessarily welcome. Certainly, this can be the case when an alcoholic or addict decides abruptly to quit drinking or using. In this chapter, we will look at some of the issues that loved ones might encounter should a substance abuser decide to stop.

▓ The Dry-Drunk Syndrome

The effects on relationships and families of addicts' decision to quit in a way that has been referred to as the "white-knuckle approach"—meaning to stop using but without any form of outside support as, for example, from AA—may be much more difficult to endure than the changes that come when an addict decides to commit him or herself to AA or NA as a means to achieve this goal. The term *dry drunk syndrome* (Solberg, 1983) was coined to refer to a constellation of personality traits associated with someone who decides to give up alcohol or drugs without seeking support and without pursuing some program of character growth and spiritual renewal, for example, through involvement in a 12-step fellowship. These programs were based in part on a recognition that the process of addiction has effects on the addict spiritually and psychologically as well as physically. One clear implication of the 12 steps is that involvement in a program such as AA can help to mitigate these effects and spare others the pain of having to live with them. It is a program of spiritual renewal as much as it is a support system for staying sober.

Dry drunks are described as follows:

> Persons who experience a full-blown dry drunk are removed from the world of sobriety; they fail to accept the necessary conditions for sober living. Their mental and emotional homes are chaotic, their approach to everyday living is unrealistic, and their behavior, both verbal and physical, is unacceptable. (Solberg, 1983, p. 3)

I have encountered more than one significant other who found themselves in the unhappy position of having to live with a dry drunk. One such person was Jill, whose husband Kevin had been forced to admit himself to a treatment center after he'd gotten into a car accident, with their two young daughters in the car, while drunk and stoned on marijuana. Jill had been aware of Kevin's drinking and pot use since they were teenagers. She had taken a tolerant attitude, in part, because she felt she had no right, to use her word, to "dictate" to him, and in part, because she also had a history of drinking and getting high, especially in her teenage years. But at 34, Jill had not smoked marijuana in over 10 years, and her drinking had decreased to the social level plus an occasional glass of red wine over dinner. Kevin, on the other hand, continued to get high every morning before he left for work and drunk every night when he got home. Though his work performance was affected by his substance abuse, he was fortunate in that he worked for a family business where he enjoyed the benefits of a certain degree of toleration born of the family's unwillingness to confront the issue. All that changed with the accident. Jill orchestrated a family meeting and had a counselor—not I—there. Kevin found himself confronted by a united front of family members who insisted that they loved him but also that he get help.

Kevin complained bitterly once he got to the treatment center. Describing it as "a Mickey Mouse operation," he complained that he couldn't relate to either the other patients or the counselors. "I need someone who hunts, who can relate to my lifestyle," he complained to Jill. He wanted to leave the treatment center after a week, but reluctantly agreed to stay for two.

When Kevin returned home, he told Jill that he realized that he did have a drinking problem and that he'd decided "not to drink, for now." Jill found the "for now" part of this response disconcerting, but she tried to focus on the positive, being grateful at least that Kevin acknowledged that he had a problem and wasn't drinking at that point.

Three weeks passed, and Kevin had stuck to his word about not drinking. But Jill was finding it hell to live with him. "He's angry all the time," she said.

When he gets home, I just try to keep the kids out of his way. *I* try to stay out of his way, too. He hardly talks to any of us. He just keeps himself busy all the time. And he hasn't approached me once for sex—not that I'm feeling all that turned on to him. I can't tell you how tense it is with him around. He acts like he's suffering so. He definitely was easier to live with when he was smoking and drinking every day. Not that I want to go back to that. I definitely don't. On the other hand, when family asks how things are going, I just tell them he isn't drinking, and they think that's great. They have no idea what our life is like these days!

It would probably be fair to say that Kevin was a dry drunk. Qualities associated with this syndrome include the following (Solberg, 1983):

Grandiosity: An exaggeration of one's importance

Judgmentalism: Prone to make value judgments—usually inappropriate—of others

Intolerance: Having no room for delay of gratification

Impulsivity: Being heedless of the ultimate consequences of one's behavior for self or others

Lack of introspection: Being self-absorbed but unable to view one's own behavior objectively or critically.

Another way to understand this constellation of personality traits is that, taken together, they reflect a decided immaturity. If one views addiction as a process that is associated psychologically with a slow but steady regression to earlier and less mature levels of development, then one could hypothesize that the adult alcoholic or addict who simply quits is, in psychodynamic terms, like a big child. This is precisely the way Jill perceived Kevin, and she said as much: "I feel like I have *three* kids now, and one of them—Kevin—is just a petulant, self-absorbed, surly adolescent."

Twelve-step fellowships, such as AA and NA, which advocate a program of spiritual renewal and character growth, can represent one way of helping addicts progress out of the infantile state that addiction leads to. Through involvement in AA or NA, the alcoholic or addict can also be confronted (and will be) by others who perceive his or her behavior for what it is. For example, Kevin may well have been told to "Get off the pity pot!" in response to his feeling sorry for himself, had he gone to AA. He would also have heard others talk about self-pity, identifying it as a dangerous form of arrogance and one that threatens recovery. But he chose not to go, and so Jill and his two young children were left to deal with him and his ignorance of how much substance abuse had affected him and how much growing he had to do. They had to live with this man who stalked around the house constantly brimming over with resentment that was like a charged cloud seeking a target for its lightning.

Fortunately, Jill had started going to Al-Anon when Kevin went into treatment. There, she found people who understood and related to what she was going through and who could share whatever wisdom they had about how they'd handled similar situations. Beyond that, she discovered a place she could vent the shame she'd been experiencing over her secret wish at times that Kevin would go back to drinking, just to reduce the level of tension in the house.

In Al-Anon, Jill found what she called a lifesaving source of sympathy and support. Simply discovering that others had gone through similar experiences as she was having, and that the dry-drunk syndrome was not only real but common in men like Kevin, provided Jill with a deep sense of relief, even as she continued to struggle with the realities of living with Kevin. Regardless of what Kevin decided to do about his drinking and drug use, she said, she was going to continue going to Al-Anon.

As the case of Jill and Kevin shows, being aware of the dry-drunk syndrome can be very useful for the practitioner who will have to work with the loved ones of alcoholics or addicts who gets sober, especially if they decide to do so without going to AA or NA. There is a good chance that coping with sobriety will be harder for loved ones to deal with if the alcoholic or addict decides to rely on willpower alone instead of using AA or NA as a means of staying sober. In such cases, the prognosis for recovery may be poorer, as well. In Kevin's case, for example, he "decided" to have some wine after about a month of sobriety. From his point of view, that month of sobriety had proven that he could indeed control his drinking. He therefore saw no further need to abstain. Within another month, however, he was back to drinking not only wine but also bourbon (his drink of choice) before dinner. He pointed out defensively to Jill that he now drank only one bourbon on the rocks, whereas before, he'd have three or four before dinner. A month after that, Jill, looking for a toy that her oldest daughter had misplaced, happened to open a cabinet in their living room. She reached in and to her surprise found herself grasping a large bottle. She pulled out a half gallon of bourbon, half empty, which she knew had not been there a week earlier.

As Kevin continued down the slope into relapse, Jill continued going to Al-Anon and staying in touch with several of the women she'd met there. She got ongoing support for her efforts to resist enabling Kevin while detaching from him. Part of the former was telling family members to talk to Kevin directly about whether he was or wasn't drinking; part of the latter was telling Kevin that if he ever drove again after drinking, with either of their daughters in the car, she would separate from him. She did this when he was sober, and she explained that it had been a difficult decision for her to make. She wanted Kevin to know, however, that she was serious about it. She hoped it would never come to that point, she explained, but she loved both Kevin and her children and would not risk losing all of them in an alcohol-related car accident.

▒ Relational Land Mines: Things to Watch Out for

The practitioner working with a loved one of a substance abuser should anticipate that sobriety will, in and of itself, upset an established status quo in the relationship with the addict—indeed, within the family as a whole. Descriptions follow of some of the issues the practitioner should be prepared to deal with.

Monitoring

This refers to any and all attempts to keep track of how much an alcoholic is drinking or an addict is using. Monitoring is a common and natural reaction to a substance abuse problem. It often leads to a good deal of nagging on the part of the client and defensive anger on the part of the substance abuser. The goal of monitoring is obvious: It is to get the drinker to drink less or the drug user to use less by letting him or her know that you know how much he or she is drinking or using.

Spouses and other loved ones who have engaged in monitoring say that it sometimes leads to a temporary reduction in substance abuse. This may be due to the substance abuser's desire to avoid such confrontations through placating or it may reflect guilt or shame induction or both. The fact that it may initially produce such effects may reinforce monitoring behavior in the loved ones of substance abusers.

Although monitoring may have an effect on drinking or drug use, that effect is typically transient. Sooner or later, the alcoholic or addict will react to it—as in the case of Kevin, cited earlier—by hiding the supply of drugs or alcohol, by drinking or using in secret, or both. Alternatively, the addict may eventually become more or less immune to the loved one's nagging. This in turn leads to frustration and eventually to feelings of failure, hopelessness, and depression in the significant other, to shame and resentment in the addict, and to alienation in the relationship.

Behaviorally oriented interventions as well as the present 12-step-oriented program agree that this form of monitoring is pretty much to be avoided. The exception might be a case where a loved one has avoided sharing his or her concern about the substance abuser's drinking or drug use. In that instance, the conspiracy of avoidance could be construed from the present perspective as enabling on the part of the significant other. In this instance, the therapist might consider coaching the client on how to break that conspiracy. Even so, ground rules for doing so would include confronting the substance abuser only when he or she is sober, doing so in as calm a manner as possible, and avoiding blowups. The loved one is also admonished to avoid ongoing monitoring and any tendency to nag at the substance abuser, because that almost always proves counterproductive.

From the 12-step perspective, monitoring the substance abuser or addict when he or she is sober is no more desirable than doing so when he or she is using but for several reasons. Here is where behavioral approaches and 12-step philosophy diverge, for behaviorists would argue that significant others should continue to monitor and reinforce reduced drinking or using through praise, favors, and other rewards (Meyers & Smith, 1995). From the perspective of Al-Anon, however, this would constitute a continuance of the loved one taking responsibility for the substance abuser's behavior. The goal of Al-Anon, in contrast, is to allow each partner—the addict and the codependent—to be responsible for (and therefore to take credit for) his or her own recovery. Because most alcoholics and addicts continue to be men and most codependents women, one might argue that the behavioral approach, with its emphasis on the significant other monitoring and reinforcing behavior, perpetuates an undesirable sex role for women.

Al-Anon and Nar-Anon clearly emphasize caring detachment as the healthiest model for a relationship. Consequently, they would no more advocate ongoing monitoring with reinforcement than they would advocate ongoing monitoring with punishment as a desirable dynamic in a relationship with an addict. The practitioner using this model would therefore be working most consistently with Al-Anon or Nar-Anon philosophy by being cautious about advocating any form of monitoring at all, be it accompanied by punishment or reward. That is not to say that some recognition of a substance abuser's sobriety is inappropriate. On the other hand, systematic monitoring with an eye toward behavior modification goes well beyond mere recognition; moreover, the recovering person will most assuredly receive much recognition from his or her fellow addicts through involvement in AA or NA. This connection to a fellowship of recovering persons, not the relationship of the addict with the loved one, should be the primary source of reinforcement for the recovering substance abuser.

Resentments

Addiction leads to alienation in relationships. Men and women who lose someone to alcoholism or drug addiction typically go through a process that begins with anxiety and concern, proceeds through frustration and anger, and ends in despair and alienation. Along the way, the loved ones of addicts are likely to experience deep senses of failure (in arresting the addiction), along with deep resentments of the alcohol or drugs (or both) that have destroyed the relationships. It is no surprise, then, that clients may find themselves experiencing not only joy but anger and resentment when their loved ones do get sober. The practitioner should be prepared to hear and deal with such feelings. The goal is to help to desensitize the shame or guilt that is associated with such feelings.

The most helpful initial response to anger in a loved one of an addict who is newly in recovery is to react with understanding (i.e., to normalize it). This can provide a great deal of relief to the clients who may feel shame that they are angry instead of happy that their loved ones are finally making an effort to stay clean or sober. Because many clients may have such feelings (and be ashamed of them), the facilitator would do well to bring the subject up. When doing so, the best approach is to indicate that such feelings are common enough as to be the rule rather than the exception. Open-ended questions preceded by a brief introduction, such as the following, can be useful in testing for resentment and shame:

> Addiction stirs up many reactions in people, such as yourself, who are close to an addict. We can feel worried and anxious when we first realize that our loved one has a problem. Usually, we try our best to get them to stop. This leads to frustration and anger and sometimes, to a sense of failure. Eventually, we can feel very alienated and hopeless. Have you ever experienced any of these feelings in your relationship?

> When an alcoholic or addict first gets into recovery, we want to be happy for them, and of course, part of us is. But then, there are still all those leftover feelings—hopelessness, anger, resentment—that we've had to more or less stuff so long as he or she was drinking or using. Often, these feelings never see the light of day while the addict is actively drinking or using; but then, we may experience them when he or she gets sober. This can be very upsetting, but it's a common reaction and really very understandable. Have you found yourself having any feelings of anger or resentment now that your loved one has stopped drinking or using?

> What have you tried to do to deal with any resentment, frustration, or anger you have that's left over from when _____ was actively drinking or using? Have you felt uncomfortable or ashamed at any time over any of these feelings?

Once feelings of resentment are acknowledged, the issue then becomes that of how to deal with them. This is best approached as a collaborative decision made by the client and the therapist. It is not necessarily easy for an alcoholic or addict to hear these feelings; on the other hand, the 12-step program includes explicit provisions for acknowledging harm done to others as a result of addiction and the need to make appropriate amends for such acts. Reassuring significant others that not only are their feelings understandable and therefore normal, but also that they can have a reasonable expectation that the addict will at some point hear them out and make amends, can help to turn destructive resentment into a productive exchange between the addict and the significant other.

However, it is also important to keep in mind that the addict may not be best able to accept or deal with a loved one's anger very early in his or her recovery. It may have to be sufficient for a time for significant others to share these feelings with the therapist and with others at Al-Anon or Nar-Anon meetings.

The following are offered as guidelines for discussing the issue of resentment and how to resolve it:

> Do you think it would it help if you could express any feelings of anger or resentment you have about having lost _____ to addiction?
>
> How would you express your resentment? What exactly would you like to say to _____?
>
> When do you think would be the best time for you to sit down with _____ and express some of these feelings you have about his or her addiction and the effect it has had on you and on your relationship? Do you think you should do this soon? If not, at what point in _____'s recovery would you do it?

Properly done, helping a significant other to unburden himself or herself of long-standing resentments can open the door to true reconciliation in the addict-codependent relationship. Ironically, many relationships seem to fail not while an addict is actively using but after she or her gets sober. One reason for this may have to do with this issue of unresolved resentments.

Jealousy

"Before he got sober, he spent all his time drinking. Now that he's sober, he spends all his time at AA meetings!" Such sentiments have been expressed by more than one spouse or child of a recovering alcoholic or addict, and they are understandable. Consider, for example, the implications for a newly recovering addict's relationships with family members of the common AA prescription to newcomers to attend 90 meetings in 90 days. An old saw within AA and NA, this "90 in 90" advice turns out to have a sound empirical basis because most relapses have been found to occur within the first 90 days after an addict stops drinking or using (Marlatt & Gordon, 1985). At the same time that it makes sense in term of recovery, though, this 90-in-90 rule can effectively mean that the recovering person may spend more time at meetings during this period than they do at home.

In addition to being asked to attend as many as 90 meetings in 90 days, the newcomer to AA or NA will be encouraged to stay after meetings to talk, to go out for coffee with others after meetings, to spend time talking to others AA members on the phone, to get a sponsor and maintain frequent contact with him or her, to read the Big Book and other literature, and so on. As much as all these activities make sense in terms of getting a good start on recovery, taken together, they also mean that the newly recovering person may seem, from the point of view of family members, to have "traded one addiction (alcohol or drugs) for another (AA or NA)," as one spouse put it.

The facilitator should be prepared to empathize with the significant other who expresses the sentiment that he or she has in essence lost the addict to a 12-step fellowship. Often, these loved ones have longed for years to have better relationships with the addicts. They may be reluctant to admit that they are in fact jealous of the recovering person's newfound relationships within AA or of the fact that these other anonymous people seem able to do what they were not (i.e., get their loved ones sober).

It would not be abnormal if spouses and other family members were to be inwardly conflicted about their own emotional reactions to the addicts' involvements in 12-step fellowships. Almost all concerned significant others truly want to support recovery and may therefore be ashamed of any jealousy they experience. As one husband said,

> What Joan is doing [staying sober] is what I've wanted, prayed, and hoped for, for years. It bothers me that I feel annoyed when she has to leave every night, and most weekend mornings, to go to meetings. She seems genuinely happy— happier than I've ever seen her—and I want to be happy for her. But sometimes, I know that I'm forcing my smile just a bit, and that I sometimes want to protest about her being gone all the time.

This husband's statement captures the internal conflict experienced by many family members when they first get what they've wished for: their loved ones in recovery. Their inner turmoil can easily be misinterpreted as ambivalence about the addicts' sobriety itself. Therapists may be tempted to conclude that the significant other would actually prefer the addict or alcoholic to continue drinking or using. This misperception has led therapists at times to theorize about some secondary gain that significant others derive from addiction and even to suggest that significant others encourage addictive behavior because of this secondary gain. But this is almost always a mistake. More often, ambivalence reflects a normal human response—jealousy—to having a relationship diluted by a loved one's intense involvement in some other activity. This can be especially true when a significant other has already lost a loved one to addiction for a prolonged period of time.

When working with family members of substance abusers, it can be helpful to raise and discuss this issue of jealousy, even while the substance abuser is still actively using, in anticipation of what the significant other might experience if the substance abuser got clean and sober. For many significant others, having therapists predict such reactions helps to normalize them and minimize subsequent feelings of guilt.

Certainly, it is appropriate to bring this issue up early in recovery if it hasn't been before. If possible, this should be done with both the recovering addict *and* the significant other(s) in a family session. Again, frank acknowledgement can help to normalize such feelings and reduce shame and guilt in those significant others who are experiencing them. It can also open a constructive dialogue about the importance of becoming active in a 12-step fellowship while not forgetting about the importance of family relationships.

If for some reason the addict is not available for a discussion of this issue with the significant other in a conjoint session, the therapist may want to use a cognitive role-playing technique with the significant other alone. Present the following scenario, and discuss how the significant other might feel and how they might respond if this situation were to arise.

Once your loved one makes a decision to get sober through AA, you might discover that she or he is suddenly going to meetings five to seven times a week, talking to other AA members every night on the phone, spending time having coffee with a sponsor, and talking a lot about AA. Although we both know very well that you want your loved one to get sober, it wouldn't be unusual for you to have a reaction to him or her getting so absorbed in AA.

How do you think you might feel in this situation?

If you have children, how do you think they might respond?

How would you talk to your recovering loved one about your feelings?

What would you expect from him or her in terms of attention to your own relationship and family?

Coping With Getting What You Wish for

The alcoholic or addict who decides to get sober and commit to a 12-step fellowship will often experience an initial wave of relief. Early recovery, with its promise of renewed hope, along with the sense of physical well being that comes with sobriety, can create what has been called a pink cloud of optimism. It is like viewing the world through rose-colored glasses. Soon enough, however, the reality sinks in: Recovery means hard work. As one counselor, in recovery herself, explained it to her client, "Recovery means more that just putting the plug in the jug. It means learning to live life and to live it on life's terms."

The point of this discussion has been that recovery, along with its blessing of sobriety, often brings with it changes that the loved ones of addicts may not have anticipated. Recovery can stir up long-suppressed feelings of anger and resentment or create jealousy in significant others. A loved one's initial response to early recovery may be something akin to the pink cloud that the addict experiences. Soon enough, however, this will wear off. The practitioner is wise to expect this and to prepare the client for it in advance whenever possible.

Addicts in early recovery can be exuberant; sometimes, they can also turn into proselytizers for 12-step fellowships. Persons who discover hope for themselves through AA or NA, and who see in the 12 steps a true pathway to spiritual renewal, may want to "share" their new discovery with family members, some of whom may be a good deal less enthusiastic about the idea than the addict is. The best advice to give to both the addict and his or her loved ones in early recovery is to encourage acceptance and tolerance: Let the addict pursue his or her program, while the rest of the family pursues whatever routes feel best for them. For many, Al-Anon will help a great deal, if they are willing to give it a try.

Advocating that family members take a "live and let live" approach to early recovery can help to minimize resentments that could eventually sabotage recovery for all. The program of intervention described here is, of course, designed to help the professional counselor facilitate recovery for the whole family using the 12-step approach. But it is important that the counselor also take an attitude of tolerance as well as understand the kinds of reactions that codependents may have when loved ones first gets sober. The facilitator should proselytize no more than should the recovering addict. Maintaining this attitude is vital if one hopes to persuade one or more family members to try out the attitudes and behaviors—in particular, caring detachment—that I am advocating here.

PART II

Facilitating Twelve-Step Family Recovery

Program Overview

THIS PART OF THE BOOK presents, in manual form, a program for working with concerned significant others of substance abusers. It is presented in this way intentionally so that it may be used as a guide in actual treatment sessions. Prototypes of the treatment program presented here have been used in randomized clinical trials with spouses, parents, grandparents, adult children, and cohabiting significant others of substance abusers. It has not been used with minor children of substance abusers.

This program is designed to initiate a process of positive change in the family system through a brief, focused intervention with one or more family members. To be effective, the intervention should therefore be used only with concerned significant others who have frequent contact with the substance abuser. Because it seeks to accomplish its goals in a relatively brief time, it is also important that the practitioner adhere to the manual format as much as possible and avoid drifting into collateral issues.

The program begins with an assessment session. For some clients, a single hour may be sufficient to complete the assessment process; on the other hand, it is not unusual for the assessment process to extend over two sessions. The program is presented as a series of topics. Like the assessment, many of these topics could be subjects of more than one treatment session. The issue of detaching versus enabling, for example, is apt to be a topic for discussion, coaching, and therapeutic work in virtually every session.

In clinical trials, this program has been implemented in 12 sessions spaced over as long a period as 6 months. Substance abusers who seek treatment as a result of this intervention with their significant others may be referred to professionals who are prepared to facilitate their involvement in Alcoholics Anonymous or Narcotics Anonymous (or both). A manual-guided program aimed at achieving that goal has been previously described by Nowinski and Baker (1998).

CHAPTER 7

Topic 1

Introduction and Assessment

T HIS INITIAL SESSION of the facilitation program has an exceptionally large agenda and may take more than a single session to complete. Its objectives are as follows:

To establish rapport between the client (significant other) and the therapist (facilitato r)

To provide an overview of the program

To obtain an impression, based on information provided by the client, of the extent of his or her loved one's alcohol or drug problem

To help the client understand what *stage* his or her loved one's drinking or drug problem has reached

To briefly assess the client's own use of alcohol or drugs

To introduce the first of the program's recovery tasks to the client

▨ Introductions

The facilitator should be prepared to spend the opening minutes of the initial session just getting acquainted with the significant other. The issue of how the client and therapist will address one another (first vs. last names) should be discussed. A point should be made to check whether the meeting time is mutually convenient and whether the client anticipates any transportation problems or other issues (e.g., child care) that might interfere with attendance and that could be worked through at the outset. Such a discussion is helpful in establishing a practical, problem-solving, and collaborative relationship between the client and the facilitator.

▓ Presenting a Program Overview

When presenting an overview of the program, it is important that the facilitator cover the following points:

Focused Treatment

The therapist should explain that the purpose of this program is to assist the significant other in coping more effectively in a relationship with an active substance abuser: to begin the process of healing the negative impact on oneself that comes from being in a close relationship with an addict and to alter the relationship with the substance abuser in ways that may eventually motivate the addict to change. Although other issues may arise during this program, one of the facilitator's main responsibilities is to follow the prescribed session format and to keep treatment focused on these goals. This focus is not intended to imply that collateral issues are trivial; rather, it is intended to help the client achieve certain specific and limited goals in a brief period of time. Additional therapy may be recommended following completion of this program; alternatively, the client may discover ways of dealing with these other issues through the course of the program.

Time-Limited Treatment

This program was designed to be delivered in approximately 12 individual sessions spaced over a period of up to 6 months. Though not originally designed as a group intervention, it is reasonable to assume that its structure is amenable to that kind of adaptation. If further treatment is desired after completion of the program, the client is probably best referred to another professional resource for that purpose so as to preserve the boundaries of this program. Also, it is hoped that as a result of the therapist's efforts, significant others will have developed networks of supportive relationships through Al-Anon or Nar-Anon by the time the program is completed, which can be used as additional sources of nonprofessional help.

It is not recommended that this program be extended over a period of time longer than 6 months or that many additional sessions be offered. In the event that limited progress has been made and a client wishes to continue, it is suggested that instead of simply continuing, a break of anywhere from 3 to 6 months be taken before resuming treatment. During that period of time, the client should be encouraged to pursue the same goals on his or her own that are the subject of the program, namely, attending Al-Anon or Nar-Anon meetings, establishing a network of contacts, using the telephone, and establishing a relationship with a sponsor. Progress in these areas should be assessed prior to setting a new therapeutic contract. The practitioner needs to be cautious that a client does not merely wish to substitute a professional relationship for active involvement in a 12-step fellowship because this is not likely to prove useful in the long run. Resistance to such involvement is an appropriate subject for any extended sessions.

Facilitation Versus Therapy

The significant other needs to know that in the context of this program, the facilitator is seen as a professional whose expertise is directed at helping that significant other understand addiction and concepts such as codependence, enabling, and detaching and in facilitating the client's involvement in a 12-step fellowship. The facilitator is an expert, but the primary means of achieving the program's goals over the long run is ideally to be found through active involvement in Al-Anon or Nar-Anon rather than through the therapeutic relationship by itself. This is not to say that this relationship is unimportant. On the contrary, clinical experience with this program suggests that many clients would either not have tried a 12-step fellowship such as Al-Anon or Nar-Anon to begin with or would not have followed through after their initial exposures to one of these fellowships without the active support and guidance of the facilitator. Rather than minimizing his or her importance as a professional, the practitioner using this program believes that bonding to Al-Anon or Nar-Anon represents a long-term solution for the client, whereas the client-therapist relationship is an important but temporary one.

Presenting an Overview of Alcohol and Drug Abuse

Once the program overview has been presented, and before beginning the alcohol or drug (or both) history, it can be helpful to briefly present some initial information about alcohol and drug use. The Institute of Medicine (1990) report is one source of such information. Findings from it can be shared with the client as a way of placing the problem of the loved one's substance abuse into a broader perspective. According to this study, approximately 20% of the adult population in the United States are nondrinkers. An additional 55% are what could be called social drinkers or nonalcoholics. These people drink but report no significant negative consequences associated with drinking. The percentage of individuals who have what could be considered problems with drinking is approximately 20%, and an additional 5% are alcoholics or people who are compulsive drinkers.

Survey data are also available relative to drug abuse. According to the National Institute on Drug Abuse's (1995) 1993 National Household Survey, 1.3 million Americans (0.6%) are current cocaine users, and 4.3% of the population are current marijuana users.

The purpose of sharing data such as these is simply to provide a context for the problem of substance abuse and for the decision of the loved one to seek help. The point is that substance abuse and addiction are significant, if not the most significant, public health problems facing the country. People seeking help through this program therefore need not feel alone or stigmatized in any way. The numbers of people in their very situation are legion. The decision to get professional help represents one that thousands of others make every day when they walk into their first Al-Anon, Nar-Anon, or Alateen meetings, when they confide in their family doctors, or when they contact therapists to get advice and guidance.

Stages of Substance Use: A Relational Model

After the preceding data are shared, the facilitator should present the following *relational model of addiction*. This model describes substance use in terms of a relationship between the user and alcohol or drugs and correlates the several stages of addiction (Nowinski, 1990) with their effects on the addict-codependent relationship.

Stage 1: Social or Experimental Substance Use

In this stage, the substance user primarily drinks or uses with others. Alcohol and drugs are used mainly as social facilitators (to "loosen up" or to "relax") or for their pleasurable effects ("getting high") or both. Although alcohol and drugs have effects on the user's emotional state, at this stage, these disappear as the alcohol or drugs are metabolized. In other words, the user subjectively returns to normal after using. Negative consequences can occur but are relatively rare and may include occasional hangovers or even a random DWI arrest. Viewed from a relational perspective, at the social stage of use, alcohol or drugs can be thought of as a *casual friend* of the user.

Substance use at this stage is not generally perceived by loved ones (e.g., spouses or children of the user) or other concerned significant others as threats to their relationships with the substance user. Consequently, substance use at the social or experimental stage is most often met with tolerance or acceptance. The exception might come from a partner who grew up in a nondrinking family, in which case, even social use—if it has any regularity—might be noticed and remarked on.

Stage 2: Instrumental Substance Use

In this stage, the individual has learned to use alcohol, drugs, or both consistently, either to create certain positive feelings (e.g., relaxation, euphoria) or else to avoid certain negative feelings (e.g., anxiety, loneliness). The former pattern is called *hedonistic* use, whereas the latter is *compensatory* in nature (Nowinski, 1990).

Instrumental drinking is the gray area that separates social drinking from problem drinking. Men and women at this stage often begin to drink or use alone as well as socially. Relationally speaking, they could be said to have developed a *relationship* with alcohol or drugs, in the sense that their connection to alcohol or drugs goes beyond a casual level and is not limited to social situations. Use at this stage is intended to manipulate affective states; to disinhibit certain behaviors, such as sex or aggression; or to overcome certain problems, such as social anxiety.

Instrumental drinkers or users rarely experience severe negative consequences as a result of use, and it would be unusual for instrumental users or drinkers to consider themselves as having substance use problems. However, significant others may begin to notice how often they drink or get high and how much they seem to look forward to it. At this stage, loved ones may begin to experience jealousy of the emerging relationship between the user and his or her substance of choice. Ironically, however, significant others who themselves were raised in alcoholic families may fail to react to substance abuse at the instrumental stage. Although one might expect them to have been sensitized by their early experiences, in fact, they often have become desensitized by it and are apt to react only when substance abuse has progressed to the next stage: habitual use. In contrast, significant others who were raised in nonaddictive families commonly perceive instrumental use as problematic and react to it as such.

This difference in the ways instrumental substance use is perceived by significant others is important clinically because it may be tempting to pathologize a codependent who appears to take a tolerant attitude toward instrumental substance use. One might hypothesize that he or she unconsciously wants the substance abuser to drink or use, or one might suppose that he or she is unconsciously re-creating his or her family of origin. Before jumping to such conclusions, however, the therapist should consider that what seems like "normal" behavior to an individual depends in large part on the context of that behavior. Social perception, in other words, is contextual. Growing up as a child in a family where shouting and arguing is common, for example, tends to predispose the individual as an adult to perceive verbal fights as essentially nonviolent and nothing to be alarmed about. In contrast, the same individual, after growing up in a conflict-avoidant family, might well perceive a verbal fight as quite violent and disturbing.

Similar contextual factors appear to play a role in determining at what point a significant other will begin to perceive drinking or drug use as problematic. Contrary to what many may expect, growing up in a family where drinking is commonplace predisposes the individual to *not* perceive a drinking problem in its early stages. Professionals may be able to promote earlier detection and prevention of addiction by educating significant others in the addiction process and by sensitizing them to cues that are symptomatic of a developing problem, such as instrumental use. To some extent, this is happening now in schools that expose children to drug education programs.

Stage 3: Problem (Habitual) Substance Use

At this stage, alcohol or drug use has progressed from being a relationship to the level of what could be called a *commitment* that the user has to his or her substance of choice. Loved ones often relate well to this analogy of problem drinking or drug use as being a commitment between the psychoactive substance and the user—a commitment that is not only intimate but one that begins to seriously compete with the user's other relationships as well as with responsibilities at work.

Children and spouses often experience *resentment* of the habitual user's committed relationship with alcohol or drugs. The user now rarely strays far from alcohol or drugs, and she or he intentionally structures social engagements, vacations, and so on in ways that ensure ready access. As one wife put it, "My husband won't go anywhere without his cooler." And a husband said of his wife, "She refuses to go on a vacation to any place that doesn't have a bar close at hand. I hate cruises; she loves them."

At the habitual stage, negative consequences of use become increasingly apparent, and these almost invariably include strained relationships. However, decreased effectiveness at work, financial problems, and declining health may also begin to become evident as habitual use progresses. Last, definite substance-use-related personality changes begin to appear. In the emotional sphere, these changes most often include a growing emotional lability, increased aggressiveness and irritability, and depression. Psychologically, the habitual user becomes progressively more self-absorbed, unreliable, and demanding—in a word, more regressed.

At the habitual stage of use, significant others experience anger and anxiety as well as frustration in getting the user to stop or reliably limit use. The user's efforts to control drinking or using amount to little more than a series of false starts ending in failure, the long-term consequence of which is lower self-esteem and increased denial. A parallel process occurs in significant others, who similarly experience failure in their efforts to arrest the problem. Not a few drift into a state of denial as well, essentially looking the other way as the substance abuser slips down the slope into addiction.

Stage 4: Compulsive Substance Use

This is the stage of classic addiction in which substance use has progressed from a commitment to a total preoccupation. At this stage, the relationship between the user and alcohol or drugs is one of *master and slave.* Psychological and physical dependence now drives the substance user. Staying intoxicated becomes the primary focus of daily living. The compulsive substance user no longer feels normal in the absence of intoxication. Sobriety is associated with acute discomfort and irritability. Therefore, intoxication is maintained continuously whenever possible. Negative consequences in terms of health, work, and relationships continue to accrue. The addict is now an extremely regressed, indeed infantile, individual who behaves in a childish manner (e.g., inability to delay gratification, low frustration tolerance, infantile egocentrism, etc.).

By the time substance use has progressed to the compulsive stage, significant others are apt to suffer from deep feelings of *alienation.* Loneliness, depression, hopelessness, and extremely low self-esteem are the most common feelings expressed by significant others of compulsive users when they seek help or first go to an Al-Anon or Nar-Anon meeting.

✳ ✳ ✳

The therapist will find that the relational model of addiction just described will have particular relevance for many significant others. It should be presented with the aim of helping clients identify where the user is with respect to his or her relationship with alcohol or drugs and also, how they have reacted to it. Understanding the course of the significant other's relationship with the substance abuser will provide a useful context for the work on caring detachment that is to follow in later sessions.

Table 7.1 can be a useful visual aid when presenting the relational model of addiction.

TABLE 7.1   Relational Model of Addiction

Stage of Use	Relationship Between User and Alcohol or Drugs	Effects on Codependents
Social-Experimental	"Casual Friendship"	Acceptance
Instrumental	"Relationship"	Jealousy
Habitual	"Commitment"	Resentment
Compulsive	"Master-Slave"	Alienation

When using the relational model shown in Table 7.1, the facilitator should begin by helping the client identify what stage of use the drinker or user is at. Talking about the psychological and emotional effects associated with the progression of addiction can help in pinpointing the stage.

Next, the facilitator should help the client to identify how the addiction process has affected his or her relationship with the user. Ask the client if she or he can identify with any of the feelings associated with each stage of use along the progression to addiction (acceptance of early use, jealousy at the instrumental stage, resentment at the habitual stage, alienation at the compulsive stage).

Therapists using this treatment guide are encouraged to use case examples frequently to illuminate the addictive process and its effects on relationships. Here is one such example:

Scott, age 65, had been a self-described "heavy drinker" since late adolescence. He'd drunk heavily and continuously through 20-odd years of marriage and recalled how his wife once told him that if he agreed to stop drinking and give her the money, she'd buy him a Cadillac at the end of a year. After his wife died, Scott used her death as an excuse to continue drinking, but in truth, he said, he drank no more or no less than ever. Using the relational model as a guide, Scott's therapist established that he had a commitment to alcohol—one that had led in the end to a good deal of resentment on the part of his wife.

A couple of years before seeking help, Scott had started dating Maggie, a woman he'd met at the local senior center. They were good companions, he said, but he had no intention of marrying again: "One time around on the merry-go-round is enough for me," he said. But the therapist questioned whether this was the only reason why Scott was keeping a distance in this relationship. She established, for example, that

Scott had definitely kept the extent of his drinking secret from Maggie. He would drink before they went out, for instance, so as to get "a head start." He would take her to restaurants that had bars, and usually at least once while they were eating, he'd excuse himself ostensibly to go to the bathroom only to stop for a quick one at the bar before returning to the table. "So it sounds to me like you still have two women in your life, Scott," his therapist said. "You have your girlfriend, Maggie, and you have your 'other girlfriend,' liquor. You take one out for dinner but then you cheat on her even when you're with her." Scott laughed uncomfortably, but he had to admit to the truth of what the therapist was saying: "It's like sneaking off from one lady to kiss another, isn't it?"

After using the relational model to help significant others identify what stage of relationship with alcohol or drugs their substance abusers are at and how it has affected their relationships, ask them to identify what stage they themselves are at with respect to alcohol and drug use and why they believe this to be the case. Be sure to ask the following questions:

- How often do you drink or use drugs? What do you drink or use?
- What is the status of your relationship with alcohol or drugs: friendship, relationship, commitment, or master-slave?" Has it ever been a stronger relationship than it is today?
- Can you identify any personal negative consequences associated with your use of alcohol or drugs at any time in the past?

Taking an Alcohol or Drug History

The next phase of the assessment session consists of gathering a brief history of the substance abuser's use according to the significant other. Of particular concern are the *progression* of use, attempts to *stop or control* use, and *negative consequences* associated with use. These can be evaluated as follows:

Progression

The facilitator should ask a series of questions aimed at determining how substance use has *changed* over the course of the relationship. Questions such as the following can be useful in creating a portrait of how far the addiction process has progressed over time:

How much did _____ drink or use when you first met him or her? How frequently did he or she or drink or use? How much did she or he drink or use? How often, and how much, does she or he drink or use now?

When did you first notice that _____ was drinking or using significantly more or more often than he or she did when you first noticed it?

Can you recall the first time you felt concerned about _____'s substance use? What prompted that concern?

When was the first time you and _____ had a conflict over his or her substance use? What did you say? How did she or he respond?

What, if any, significant events were associated with increases in _____ 's substance use? For example, were any of the following events associated with increases in substance use?

Job changes

Marital conflict

Losses (deaths, moves)

Illnesses

Traumas (accidents, etc.)

Financial problems

Attempts to Stop or Control Use

The therapist should now inquire as to the significant other's awareness of any efforts that the user has made to stop or control substance use:

Has _____ ever tried to stop (or limit) substance use? What did she or he do to try to stop (or limit) use? How long was she or he successful either at not using at all or controlling (limiting) use?

Has _____ ever gone to AA or NA? How many times? What did she or he seem to think of AA or NA? Was she or he able to stop or cut down on substance use at that time?

Have you been aware of any efforts on _____'s part to control substance use?

Has she or he tried to drink or use only at certain times, such as evenings or weekends, without success?

Has she or he sworn off certain kinds of liquor or drugs, again, without success?

Has _____ ever gone for treatment (either inpatient or outpatient) for his or her substance use problem? If so, when and where? What was the outcome of that treatment?

Inventory of Negative Consequences

To conclude this succinct alcohol or drug history, the therapist should take some time to construct an inventory of negative consequences that the substance abuser has experienced as a result of his or her substance use. To gather this information, the facilitator and the client should go through the following list together and discuss to what extent either the substance abuser or the client has experienced any of the following consequences of substance abuse:

Physical Consequences

Make an effort to identify all medical problems, including accidents or injuries, that have affected the substance abuser, as well as stress-related illnesses that the significant other may have experienced. Discuss which of these problems, in either the user or the codependent, could be related in whole or in part to the substance use problem. A partial list of problems to consider includes the following:

Hypertension (high blood pressure)

Gastrointestinal (digestive) problems

Sleep disorders: insomnia; restless sleep

Weight loss or gain

Auto, home, or job accidents or injuries

Injuries suffered as a result of domestic violence

Emergency room visits

Heart problems

Liver disease

Overdoses

Legal Consequences

Compile a list of all legal consequences correlated with substance abuse, including but not limited to the following:

DWI arrests

Arrests for disorderly conduct (including domestic violence)

Arrests for possession of drugs or drug paraphernalia

Social Consequences

The facilitator should carefully inventory all social consequences of substance abuse, both to the addict and the codependent, including these:

Loss of friends

Alienation from or conflict with family members that are related to the substance abuse problem

Marital conflict

Parenting problems: underachievement, defiance, substance abuse in children, or a combination of these

Child abuse

Sexual Consequences

Though seldom discussed, substance abuse is commonly associated with sexual dysfunction and other sexual consequences. Ask about sexual dysfunction and other sexual consequences related to substance abuse that have affected the codependent or the substance abuser. These may include the following:

Problems of arousal (e.g., impotence in men, dyspareunia in women)

Orgasmic dysfunction (anorgasmia in women, delayed ejaculation in men)

Loss of sexual desire

Sexual victimization or exploitation (e.g., rape)

Psychological Consequences for the Significant Other

Ask the significant other about any symptoms of psychological disorder or stress that he or she may be experiencing. Though more inclined by habit to focus on their substance abusers, significant others also commonly experience emotional and psychological problems, such as the following:

Depression, as reflected in these symptoms:

Irritability or moodiness

Hopelessness

Loss of motivation

Insomnia or disturbed sleep (e.g., waking up consistently in the middle of the night, trouble getting to sleep)

Anxiety attacks

Overeating or undereating

Psychological Consequences for the Substance Abuser

Take an inventory of psychological and emotional problems that the substance abuser may be experiencing as a result of substance abuse, including the following:

Memory problems (especially forgetfulness)

Impulsivity

Aggressiveness or chronic irritability

Impatience and low tolerance for frustration

Confused thinking

Moodiness and periods of depression

Financial Consequences

Ask the codependent specifically about the impact that substance abuse has had on the addict's financial status, including the following:

Job problems: losing raises, being fired or placed on probation, being passed over for a promotion

Money spent on alcohol or drugs: How much does the substance abuser spend on alcohol or drugs per week? Per month? Per year?

Out-of-pocket costs for alcohol or drug treatment

Costs of impulse buying related to substance abuse

Creditor problems: overextended credit, revoked credit cards, and so forth

Mortgage or rent delinquencies

Fines and legal fees associated with alcohol-related or drug-related arrests.

▨ Summing Up

The therapist should use the information gathered through this part of the interview to summarize the impact that substance abuse has had on both the user and the significant other. Take pains to avoid minimizing in any way the negative impact that substance abuse has had on significant others' physical health, emotional health, sexuality, finances, and so on and the need for them to take care of themselves.

As a consequence of the fact that it is the progression of addiction in the alcohol or drug user—as opposed to the respective needs of each person in the relationship—that becomes the primary focus in the addict-codependent relationship, many codependents develop a long-standing habit of neglecting themselves and their own needs. Many suffer from significant psychological, physical, emotional, and spiritual problems. Failure to clearly point out the effects of addiction on significant others may undermine their motivation to change the ways they relate to their substance abusers, which is central to this intervention.

For many clients, being asked to go to meetings, as they are asked to do in this program, may be perceived initially as yet another responsibility in what may well be an already overburdened life. Some may regard Al-Anon or Nar-Anon as something else they have to do "for the addict," and therefore, resent it. A primary goal of this program is to shift the focus away from the substance abuser to the significant other and specifically, to his or her physical and mental health, including his or her unmet social needs, in the belief that as a codependent's priorities and behavior change, so will the addict-codependent relationship.

The summary is a good time to make the following points:

◆ The first point is that a goal in this program is to help the significant other focus more on his or her own needs and less on those of the substance abuser— or at least to help the significant others see how addiction has affected them and how they, as well as the substance abuser, need help. Substance abuse creates an imbalance in the relationship between the needs of the significant other and those of the substance abuser. There is a need to restore some balance in the relationship. Many significant others are prone to minimize their own problems and to believe these problems would disappear if the substance abuser simply got clean and sober. Experience teaches that this is not the case. The problems that result from being in a close relationship with an addict tend to become ingrained and require attention in and of themselves.

◆ The second point is that the best way to promote positive change in the substance abuser over the long run is for the significant other to assess and care for his or her own needs, thereby changing in a fundamental way how he or she relates to the addict.

It has been pointed out that significant others often build up considerable resentment toward the substance abusers. This comes in part from their frustrations in getting the substance abusers to stop drinking or drug use and in part from the aforementioned imbalance in the relationship. As much as they may want to let go of the substance abusers and focus on their own needs, many significant others feel guilty doing so (i.e., that that would be selfish), feel anxious about what would happen if they did so, or both. The therapist using this program needs to clearly and repeatedly challenge such thinking, emphasizing how caring detachment will prove to be the best course for both the user and the significant other in the long run. Here is a case example:

◆

Tina had been married to Glenn for 8 years. Throughout their marriage, he had abused heroin. He was employed as a health-care professional, but due mainly to his substance abuse problem, he had failed three times to pass a certification exam that would have led to a substantial increase in salary. In addition, his drug habit had led them into a series of financial crises. Each time, Tina had been the one to work harder to bail them out.

Tina also had a 16-year-old sister, Marie, who'd been living with her and Glenn for a year. Marie had moved in after her and Tina's mother had remarried and moved out of state, because she did not want to leave the high school she was in. Marie could be very oppositional and strong willed, and like Glenn, she demanded a great deal of Tina's time and attention. She would not easily follow rules or help out around the house; on the other hand, she was not shy to ask for money, the use of Tina's car, and so forth.

When first asked about herself, Tina just smiled and shrugged, as if to minimize the cumulative effects on her of the stress she'd been under as a result of Glenn's substance abuse problem plus having to be a surrogate mother to a rebellious teenager. Through the assessment, however, it was learned that she'd been chronically tired for at least 3 years. Typically, she was in bed and asleep by 9:00 and had to be up by 5:00 to get ready for work herself and to rouse both Glenn and Marie. In the past 2 years, she'd missed more days from work on account of illness than she'd missed in the previous 10 years combined. She had lost any sexual desire a "long time ago." At one time committed to physical fitness, she couldn't remember the last time she'd exercised regularly. And in the previous year, she'd gained 10 pounds.

Psychologically, spiritually, and emotionally, Tina was not well. Her self-esteem was very low, as manifested in frequent self-derogatory remarks, for instance, about not being competent at being either a wife or a surrogate mother. She was clearly aware of being treated with a lack of respect and consideration but felt helpless to change her situation. In her mind, it was as though she was fated to be abused. Not surprisingly, she scored as moderately high on a standard measure of depression. She wasn't sure where her life was heading, and she felt hopeless and adrift.

Tina's original motivation for seeking help reflected her despair: "I thought you might have some answers for me. I'm sure I'm doing something wrong, but I can't figure out what I should be doing instead."

Following the assessment, Tina's therapist took a few minutes to summarize how the stresses and frustrations of her relationships with Glenn and Marie had taken their toll on her. The therapist went on to suggest that part of what Tina might have to learn was how "less is more,"—how taking better care of herself might in fact prove to be the best way to change things in her family. Tina had a hard time seeing this at first, but she agreed that because her way had not been working, she was willing to place her trust in the therapist for awhile.

The summary, though brief, capitalized on information that Tina herself supplied. It proved to be influential in facilitating Tina's initial willingness to follow therapeutic recommendations. These recommendations were surprisingly simple, yet they turned out to be highly effective: Tina was encouraged to take two evenings a week—one to attend a Nar-Anon meeting and one to go to the health club where she had a long-neglected lifetime membership. She was encouraged and coached on how not to let anything interfere with her participation in these two activities. Last, she was told not to prepare dinner in advance for Glenn and Marie on these evenings.

Her therapist predicted that Tina could expect to encounter resistance about being out two nights a week, in the form of discouragement and complaining from her husband and her sister, and prepared her for it. Tina was told that this was to be expected as she took these first steps toward what the therapist called caring detachment. She and the counselor role-played these situations, and Tina was therefore prepared for them when they happened. Without this support—from both her therapist and the friends she was beginning to make at Nar-Anon—Tina said she doubted that she would have had the courage to persevere and probably would have given in and given up both Nar-Anon and the health club to stay home and take care of Glenn and Marie.

During one of her sessions, Tina described how her relationships with Glenn and Marie had started to change. Before she did this, however, she told her therapist how much better she was beginning to feel about herself. She'd lost five pounds and was beginning to recover some of her lost energy. She said that Glenn had been complaining a lot over the past month about her going to Nar-Anon meetings, which she'd increased to two per week. She'd told him that she found them very helpful and would not stop going. On at least two occasions, she said, she'd flatly refused to "lend" him money, knowing very well it would go for drugs. "Last night he said to me, 'I want my old Tina back.' I actually laughed. I said, 'Well, this is the new Tina, so you might as well get used to her.' "

On the day before this interaction with Glenn, Marie had asked Tina if she could use her car to meet some friends. "Not tonight," Tina had replied, "it's my workout night." Marie frowned. At one time, she would have argued and maybe even cursed Tina out, but this time, she offered no back talk, for she knew somehow that Tina meant what she said. This little exchange marked a turning point in Tina's relationship with Marie.

This case example illustrates how family recovery can begin with the recovery of one member. That member may not be the one with the substance abuse problem; on the contrary, it may be one of the most healthy members of the family. The change process begins when a significant other realizes that addiction has affected him or her and that there is a need to start taking care of his or her own physical, emotional, and spiritual well-being. The family system begins to change as this person relates to themselves differently and, consequently, to others differently, as in the case of Tina.

Introducing Recovery Tasks

Before ending this initial session, the facilitator should introduce the concept of recovery tasks and ask the client to follow through on two such initial tasks.

Recovery tasks consist of concrete suggestions made by the facilitator that are intended to educate the codependent in key 12-step concepts, engage him or her in a collaborative relationship with the facilitator, and facilitate the process of bonding to Al-Anon or Nar-Anon. Recovery tasks are given at the end of each session and followed up on at the outset of the next session.

For the assessment session, the facilitator should begin by explaining that recovery tasks, although not required, are intended to promote clear thinking and to help the client decide how to redefine his or her relationship to the addict. Indicate that there will be no negative consequences if the client does not follow through on a particular recovery task; on the other hand, you will routinely follow up to see if these tasks have raised any issues or questions. Explain that following through on recovery tasks will enhance the effectiveness of treatment by providing experiences that will make these treatment sessions more useful.

Explain that recovery tasks will typically include these four things:

1. Suggested Al-Anon or Nar-Anon meetings to attend
2. Suggested readings
3. Suggested things to do to feel more a part of Al-Anon or Nar-Anon
4. Suggestions for how to begin to detach in a caring way from the substance abuser

Explain that recovery tasks represent a collaboration between yourself as the facilitator and the client. As an experienced professional, you will have some specific ideas for things the client could do between sessions in each of the mentioned areas. However, it is also important that the client become an active participant in the process of determining recovery tasks.

Treatment Note: Journaling

Journaling can be a useful method for enhancing the effectiveness of this intervention. For those clients who have prior experience in keeping a journal or diary, as well as for those who are open to the idea, journaling is highly recommended. The facilitator may wish to provide the client with a composition book for this purpose. Explain that you would like the client to use this journal to write down his or her thoughts about any of the recovery tasks that she or he does as well as any other significant thoughts or questions that occur between sessions. Explain that the journal is a private one that you will not read, but you will ask the client to talk about any journal entries she or he feels comfortable sharing, at the beginning of each session.

Readings

For this first session, ask the client to read Chapter 1: "Bill's Story" and Chapter 8: "To Wives" from *Alcoholics Anonymous* (AA, 1976) or Chapter 1: "Who Is an Addict?" from *Narcotics Anonymous* (NA, 1985) or all three. If the substance abuser uses *only* alcohol, then the reading from *Narcotics Anonymous* may be omitted. Explain that although these first readings are from AA and NA literature, future readings will also come from the book, *Al-Anon Faces Alcoholism* (Al-Anon, 1985). Tell the client that you plan to discuss any reactions to these readings at the next session, and ask him or her to write down any reactions and thoughts the journal if she or he has agreed to keep one. Again, here are the recommended readings:

Alcoholics Anonymous (AA, 1976), Chapter 1: "Bill's Story"; Chapter 8: "To Wives"

Narcotics Anonymous (NA, 1985), Chapter 1: "Who Is an Addict?"

Treatment Note: Talking With Husbands About Chapter 8

Chapter 8 was written by the wife of a recovering alcoholic and was included in *Alcoholics Anonymous* (AA, 1976) as advice to spouses. As such, it could easily have been titled "To Spouses." It is important to explain to male clients that it applies just as much to husbands as it does to wives.

Treatment Note: Deciding on Suggested Readings

The facilitator will need to use his or her judgment when deciding whether to recommend readings from AA, NA, or both. Even when the user is solely a drug abuser, some readings from the AA Big Book, especially Chapter 8, are still relevant. Also, readings from the text, *Al-Anon Faces Alcoholism* (Al-Anon, 1985), are applicable regardless of the nature of the addiction, because the concepts of enabling and detaching are generic ones.

Meetings

Because Al-Anon and Nar-Anon will be discussed in detail in Session 2, the facilitator may decide not to suggest that the client attend any Al-Anon or Nar-Anon meetings at this point unless the client has had some prior experience with Al-Anon or Nar-Anon and feels positively about that experience and also expresses a willingness to go to one or more meetings. The facilitator should test this out straightforwardly: Ask the client if she or he knows what Al-Anon or Nar-Anon is, if he or she has had any experience with either one of these fellowships, and if so, what that experience was like.

If the response to this inquiry is positive, the facilitator can ask the client how she or he would feel about attending one or two Al-Anon or Nar-Anon meetings between sessions. If the client is open to this, give him or her a current Al-Anon or Nar-Anon meeting schedule (or both) and spend a few minutes identifying one meeting that would be convenient for the client to attend. Ask the client to write down any reactions to any meetings attended in his or her journal.

If the facilitator detects ambivalence or a frankly negative reaction to this initial inquiry, defer any further discussion or recommendations about meetings until you have had a chance to discuss Al-Anon and Nar-Anon and explore these negative reactions more completely.

CHAPTER 8

Topic 2

Principles of Twelve-Step Fellowships

I N THIS SESSION, the therapist reviews the client's reactions to the assessment process and initial recovery tasks, discusses with the client some basic
assumptions shared by 12-step fellowships, and attempts to actively facilitate the
client's initial use of Al-Anon or Nar-Anon or both.

Beginning with this session, all treatment sessions should follow this format:
review of previous session, recovery tasks, and journal; presentation and discussion of *new material*; and discussion of new *recovery tasks.*

▓ Review

Like most psychotherapists, those practitioners who use this program will
typically begin a session with a general inquiry into how the client's life has been
going since the last session. Although appropriate, this checking-in process
should not be permitted to grow into a lengthy digression that leaves little time
left for the core material presented here.

To underscore the importance of recovery tasks in this program, the therapist should be sure to include in the opening part of this and every subsequent
session some discussion of the client's reactions not only to what was discussed
in the last session but also to any readings that she or he did or meetings that she
or he attended. Also, ask the client to share any journal entries that she or he feels
comfortable sharing.

◼ New Material

The facilitator should attempt to cover as much of the following material as possible. *It is very important, however, to be sure to leave 5 to 10 minutes at the end of this (and every) session for the discussion of recovery tasks.* Therefore, if all of the issues in the following list cannot be adequately covered with enough time left for recovery tasks, it is best to stop at some point, discuss recovery tasks, and continue the discussion of this topic at the next session.

AA, NA, Al-Anon, and Nar-Anon all share a common view of addiction and recovery. The principles that guide them are described in their respective publications, but it is helpful to introduce them in an organized way early on with the client, in an effort to make certain that she or he has a basic understanding of them even before stepping into a meeting.

An accurate understanding of 12-step fellowships and how they work can help to alleviate anxieties and motivate the significant other to try Al-Anon or Nar-Anon as well as enhance their abilities to make optimum use of them. Conversely, to the extent that negative attitudes about AA, NA, Al-Anon, or Nar-Anon are based on misconceptions, false stereotypes, or prejudice, motivation to even give Al-Anon or Nar-Anon a try may be seriously undermined.

Begin by reading aloud the following excerpts from Chapter 8 of *Alcoholics Anonymous* (AA, 1976) and ask the client to share his or her reactions:

> Our loyalty and the desire that our [spouses] hold up their heads and be like other [people] have [gotten us into] all sorts of predicaments. We have been unselfish and self-sacrificing. We have told innumerable lies to protect our pride and our [spouses'] reputations. We have prayed, we have begged, we have been patient. We have struck out viciously. We have run away. We have been hysterical. We have been terror stricken. Our homes have been battlegrounds many an evening. (p. 105)

> As animals on a treadmill, we have patiently and wearily climbed, falling back in exhaustion after each futile effort to reach solid ground. (p. 107)

After reading these passages aloud, ask the codependent the following questions:

> Can you identify personally with any of these statements?

> In what ways has your relationship been like the one described?

> Do you ever feel frustrated or exhausted as a result of your loved one's substance use problem?

This kind of discussion provides a useful lead-in to the material that should now be presented.

In this session, the therapist seeks to engage the client in a frank and open-ended discussion of the following basic assumptions underlying the 12-step fellowships of AA, NA, Al-Anon, and Nar-Anon.

Loss of Control

AA, NA, and other 12-step fellowships are founded on the notion that substance abuse progresses—from social use through habitual use to compulsive use. The problem drinker or drug user progressively loses control over his or her ability to limit substance use. The following passage from *Alcoholics Anonymous* (AA, 1976) captures the essence of loss of control:

> Here are some of the methods we have tried: Drinking beer only, limiting the number of drinks, never drinking alone, never drinking in the morning, drinking only at home, never having it in the house, never drinking during business hours, drinking only at parties, switching from scotch to brandy, drinking only "natural" wines, agreeing to resign if ever drunk on the job, taking a trip, . . . (p. 31)

Narcotics Anonymous (NA, 1985) describes addiction in this way:

> Do we understand that we have no real control over drugs? Do we recognize that in the long run, we didn't use drugs—they used us? Do we fully accept the fact that our every attempt to stop using or to control our using failed? (p. 18)

The point in these statements is simple but clear: *Addiction implies loss of control, and loss of control means the progressive defeat of personal willpower.* As the addict moves from being a Type 1 drinker or user to a Type 4 drinker or user, as described in Chapter 8 of *Alcoholics Anonymous* (AA, 1975, pp. 108-110), she or he goes through an intense private struggle to limit or stop substance use. Despite occasional periods of sobriety, over the long run, the alcoholic or addict cannot reliably predict or control how much he or she will drink or use. As an AA saying has it, "No alcoholic wants *one* drink." Sooner or later, cravings overcome even the best of intentions, and the alcoholic or addict goes on a binge.

With each successive failure to control or limit use, self-esteem suffers more. The alcoholic or addict, unwilling to face the truth—that personal willpower is not working—either denies that the problem exists or else insists that she or he is still in control.

The first step of Alcoholics Anonymous as well as Narcotics Anonymous is a statement of acceptance of this loss of control over substance use. Taking this step is a major struggle for many addicts, who view it (correctly) as a defeat (of individual willpower). Their denial reflects their unwillingness to face up to this simple yet stark reality: that they cannot stop or effectively control substance use on their own.

Loss of control in addicts has its parallels in codependents. In fact, the first step of Al-Anon and Nar-Anon is identical to the first step of AA and NA: "We admitted we were powerless over alcohol—that our lives had become unmanageable" (Al-Anon, 1985, p. 236)

Using the foregoing as talking points, the therapist should engage the client in a discussion of loss of control in the substance abuser, using questions such as the following:

In what ways has your loved one tried to limit or stop his or her substance use?

Describe the loss-of-control process as you've observed it in your loved one.

How has your loved one tried to avoid facing up to his or her powerlessness over alcohol or drugs?

Next, apply the loss-of-control concept to the client, inquiring with questions such as these:

Have you believed that you could somehow get your loved one to either reliably limit or stop substance use?

Have you believed that your willpower alone could be enough to help your loved one overcome his or her substance use problem?

Have you ever believed that if you just tried hard enough, you could get your loved one to stop substance use?

Have you ever felt out of control or powerless when it came to your loved one's substance use?

Denial

Denial was touched on earlier. It is nicely summarized in the description of the types of drinkers found in Chapter 8 of *Alcoholics Anonymous* (AA, 1976). Here are some excerpts:

Type One: Your [spouse] may be only a heavy drinker. . . . It may be slowing him [her] down, but he [she] does not see it.

Type Two: Your [spouse] is showing lack of control. . . . He [she] often gets entirely out of hand when drunk. He [she] admits this is true, but is positive that he [she] will do better.

Type Three: He [she] admits he [she] cannot drink like other people, but does not see why. He [she] clings to the notion that he [she] will find a way to do so. (pp. 108-110)

The same process applies, of course, to drug abuse. Denial is an integral part of addiction because it reflects the tendency, shared by most people in our culture, to resist accepting limitations on personal power. It has been suggested that our culture is heavily influenced by a social philosophy of *radical individualism* (Bellah, Madsen, Sullivan, Swidler, & Tipton, 1985; Room, 1993). This ethic is based on a premise of extreme self-determination: We are the masters of our ships, the captains of our souls. As a result of this cultural bias, many men and women in our society are reluctant to accept the idea that they can be out of control of anything or the idea that they cannot overcome any problem through personal willpower alone. Such attitudes represent so-called rugged individualism in the extreme.

Although denial will be the topic for a future session, it is recommended that the therapist briefly test the waters now with regard to whether the client has a basic understanding of the concept, using questions such as the following:

Can you relate to any of these quotations? In what ways has your loved one resisted facing up to the fact that she or he was losing control over substance use?

Why do you think your loved one might not want to admit that she or he can't control substance use?

As in the earlier discussion of loss of control, apply the concept of denial also to the client, using questions such as these:

How hard has it been for *you* to admit that your loved one was losing control over his or her substance use?

Have you found yourself not wanting to admit that you cannot make your loved one stop using alcohol or drugs?

Spirituality and Fellowship Versus Personal Willpower

If individual willpower alone cannot overcome addiction, then what can? Twelve-step fellowships such as AA, NA, Al-Anon, and Nar-Anon are based on the idea that alcoholism and drug addiction can be overcome by turning to the resources of a Higher Power. This Higher Power may be a Judeo-Christian conception of God, as it is for many, or it may be some other spiritual belief. Alternatively, it may be embodied in the fellowship of AA or NA itself. Any or all of these things can be construed as being stronger and wiser than the individual addict struggling on his or her own to maintain control.

The therapist should introduce this idea of a power greater than individual willpower, elaborating on it by making the following three points.

First, although recovery for both the addict and the significant other begins by admitting powerlessness over alcohol or drugs, this does *not* mean that either one is *helpless.* There is, in other words, an important difference between loss of control over substance use and helplessness to do anything about it. What AA and NA ask alcoholics and addicts to do as a first step toward recovery is to give up any illusions they harbor that they can successfully control substance use and instead, accept the need to give it up. Next, AA and NA ask those who want to stop drinking or using to reach out for help beyond themselves.

Similarly, what Al-Anon and Nar-Anon ask of significant others is to stop trying to control or protect the drinker or user. Substance abusers can do something about their substance abuse if they are willing to accept the problem and follow the program outlined in the 12 steps. But to the extent that significant others protect the addict, the addict will not be likely to face up to his or her powerlessness over substance use or be motivated to change.

The second point is that on a spiritual level, both the addicts and their significant others must ultimately find the faith to believe that the problem of alcoholism or drug addiction can be overcome. This faith stands in opposition to the cynicism and despair that result from repeated failure to control or stop use without outside support. *Does the client have any hope at this point that his or her loved one's substance abuse problem can be overcome by reaching out to others?*

Third, on a practical level, AA, NA, Al-Anon, and Nar-Anon ask that we place ourselves in the hands of a fellowship and allow the collective wisdom of the group to guide our actions. This is of course a profound issue of trust that both addicts and their significant others must ultimately confront. *Is the client willing to trust others who have walked this path before, enough to reserve judgment and follow their advice?*

✳ ✳ ✳

Ask the client to share his or her reactions to each of the foregoing ideas. It is not necessary to seek a heartfelt commitment to these concepts at this time, much less to try to change the client's beliefs. On the contrary, therapists should avoid taking any positions that could be perceived as proselytizing or criticizing. Rather, the objective here is to introduce these ideas and ascertain whether the client understands them in a basic way and how she or he reacts to them on a gut level. This dialogue will help the therapist to identify areas of potential resistance to basic 12-step concepts that may be the subject of future sessions.

Treatment Note: Discussing Higher Power

Introducing the concept of a Higher Power definitely does *not* mean that this subject should be allowed to turn into a protracted discussion, much less a debate, between the client and the therapist over their respective religious preferences or spiritual beliefs. This writer, for example, once supervised a practitioner who quite seriously asked a client, in their first session, the following question when introducing the concept of a Higher Power: "You don't have any problem with organized religion, do you?"

In approaching discussions about Higher Power, it helps if the therapist is reasonably clear in his or her own mind about his or her own spiritual beliefs and comfortable with them. Second, it is helpful if she or he is comfortable with divergent beliefs, including varied ways of thinking about God. With respect to 12-step fellowships and spirituality, the therapist must understand that by tradition, they are pluralistic, not dogmatic, in their interpretation of the concept of Higher Power. Bill Wilson, for example, stated: "You can, if you wish, make AA itself your 'higher power.' In this respect they are certainly a power greater than you, who have not even come close to a solution" (Al-Anon, 1985, p. 27).

What is primary at this time is not the client's particular views of God or his or her religiosity; rather, what matters is that the client understands that AA and NA, and Al-Anon and Nar-Anon, challenge us to have hope that recovery can occur and also to place our trust in others who have struggled with similar issues before us. Collectively, these personal qualities—hope and trust—could be said to be an important part of our spirituality. The particular Higher Power that the addict or the significant other chooses to place their faith in may be a traditional concept of God. Alternatively, one's Higher Power may be the wisdom of a group conscience, which was described by Bill Wilson, cofounder of AA, in this way:

> We believe that every AA group has a conscience. It is the collective conscience of its own membership. Daily experience informs and instructs this conscience. . . . As this process continues, the group becomes better able to receive right direction for its own affairs. Trial and error produces group experience, and out of corrected experience comes custom. . . . The Greater Power is then working through a clear group conscience. (Bill W., 1948/1992)

What seems most apparent from both of the previous quotations is that addicts are challenged in AA and NA to abandon individual willpower in favor of the group and also, that 12-step fellowships have placed their faith in a kind of cultural evolution: the incremental development of a body of common wisdom and custom built on collective experience and community. This may well explain why some addicts report that going to AA or NA constituted their first experience of connectedness. The same applies to many significant others, who similarly describe Al-Anon and Nar-Anon as their "family."

Spiritual Renewal

Twelve-step fellowships recognize that addiction has progressively negative effects on self-esteem, faith, hope, and relationships. These are all facets of what we could call the *human spirit*. In Al-Anon and Nar-Anon, in particular, members are encouraged to pay attention to their own emotional, social, and spiritual needs; to focus less on the addicts in their lives; and to detach from efforts to control or protect the addicts. If the addict is to change, Al-Anon and Nar-Anon believe, that change is more likely to come indirectly—the result of the codependent's increasing detachment—than from efforts to directly control or shield the addict.

Ask the client now to summarize in his or her own words how being in a relationship with an addict has affected his or her own spirituality. As a guide, inquire briefly into each of these facets of spirituality:

Self-esteem: Feelings of personal worth and competence—what one has to offer to the world in general and one's value to others

Faith: Belief in the meaningfulness of life and in a power greater than the self

Hope: Optimism versus pessimism; a belief that things can get better

Relationships: Sense of connectedness to others, versus alienation

Though hardly an inclusive definition of spirituality, the foregoing can lead to a fruitful initial dialogue. It raises issues that will prove relevant to the significant other's ability to bond to a fellowship. Again, this initial discussion need not be lengthy or exhaustive; rather, at this time, the therapist is checking to see that the client has a basic understanding of these ideas and testing the client's gut reactions to them. Generally speaking, the more the individual's spirit has been wounded through addiction, the more reticent they will be to place their faith in others again.

▓ Recovery Tasks

The following are suggested as recovery tasks for the codependent to be completed prior to the next session:

Readings

Ask the client if she or he would be willing to read the following material prior to the next session. Include readings from *Narcotics Anonymous* (NA, 1985) and the NA pamphlet only if the client is in a relationship with a drug abuser.

Alcoholics Anonymous (AA, 1976), Chapter 2: "There Is a Solution"; Chapter 3: "More About Alcoholism"

Al-Anon Faces Alcoholism (Al-Anon, 1985), pages 91-103: "Serenity Does Not Depend on Sobriety"; "Living With Al-Anon"; "We Learn to Live"; "Perfectly Good People Get Alcoholism"; "The Face of an Angel"

Narcotics Anonymous (NA, 1985), Chapter 2: "What Is the Narcotics Anonymous Program?"; Chapter 3: "Why Are We Here?"

NA pamphlet, *Am I an Addict?* (NA, 1983)

Meetings

If this was not done at the end of the assessment session, now is the time to suggest to the client that she or he try going to one or two Al-Anon or Nar-Anon meetings (or both). The discussions just mentioned will hopefully have been helpful in preparing the client for this suggestion. In addition, it is helpful if the therapist has on hand current Al-Anon and Nar-Anon meeting schedules covering the geographic area where the client lives.

If the client has had some prior exposure to Al-Anon or Nar-Anon and if this exposure was basically a positive experience, suggest that the client give it a try again now, this time, using the relationship with the therapist as a vehicle for processing the new experience. *If you have one, give the client a current meeting schedule and help him or her identify a couple of meetings that would be convenient.* If she or he is keeping a journal, ask that she or he also take a few minutes to write down reactions to any meetings attended. Remind the client that it is perfectly acceptable to just go and listen at meetings (i.e., that they may choose not to talk much at first).

If the client appears resistant to the idea of going to Al-Anon or Nar-Anon, be sure to listen carefully to ascertain whether this reaction is based on actual experience at meetings versus stereotypes, prejudice, or misinformation about

12-step fellowships. If negative attitudes seem to be based on preconceived notions, as opposed to actual experience, it can be helpful to ask the client to share his or her image of Al-Anon and Nar-Anon: *What kinds of people do you imagine would go to an Al-Anon or Nar-Anon meeting, and what do you think happens there?* Engage the client in a discussion of his or her stereotypes and the expectations that arise from them. Stereotypes and prejudices can easily undermine a significant other's motivation to give a 12-step fellowship a try. Many times, these prejudices can be reduced if they are simply discussed openly.

Negative feelings based on actual experience often have their roots in disappointed expectations. Some people may have gone to one or more Al-Anon meetings hoping for quick solutions to their problem—for a way to get the alcoholic or addict in their lives to stop—only to be sorely disappointed when they discover a group of people who speak about detaching from the addict. Many people misconstrue detaching to mean rejection of the addict; not a few have said that they interpreted this talk to mean that they should divorce. Reticent to ask questions, they never clarified their misconceptions. Feeling frustrated and disappointed, they ended up feeling worse after going to a meeting. "It made me feel depressed and hopeless to be with a group of people who seemed to be sitting in the same sinking boat as I was in, with no solution in sight," is what one significant other wrote in her journal after her first Al-Anon meeting.

Disappointment can also be the result when someone's initial exposure to Al-Anon or Nar-Anon is less than encouraging—for example, if members at a particular meeting share experiences that are considerably less than upbeat. Another significant other expressed dismay when she learned that some members of the Al-Anon meeting she attended had been going there for 10 years. "I can't imagine doing that for 10 years," she said. In response, the therapist pointed out that this woman's husband had already been an alcoholic for nearly *15* years. Moreover, some significant others continue going to Al-Anon even after their loved one has become sober or after their relationship has ended, simply because they find it rewarding. This disappointed newcomer was advised to get to know not only this one group but several others much better before reaching a judgment about how helpful Al-Anon might be. By doing nothing different, the therapist said, the client could reasonably expect nothing to change for the better (i.e., the relational status quo would go on ad infinitum). On the other hand, by getting involved in Al-Anon now, even after 15 years in an alcoholic marriage, and by starting to take care of her own emotional, social, and spiritual needs, there was good reason to hope that many things could change for the better in the future, both for herself and in her marriage. Detachment may take time, but it is ultimately productive for the loved ones of addicts, regardless of whether or not the substance abuser continues to drink or use.

A final example: The wife of an alcoholic went to her first Al-Anon meeting only to find that the group was small, that the members much older than she was, and that they sat around a large table. She said that she tried to ignore these issues and concentrate instead on what was being said. But she left the meeting feeling unsatisfied. Her therapist reassured her that she could understand this reaction, saying the meeting sounded more formal than most. The therapist then pointed out that no two Al-Anon meetings were identical. "There is really no such thing as a 'standard' Al-Anon meeting," she said. "There are many different meetings, and each one varies depending on what the group wants. So maybe we need to scout out some different meetings for you to try out."

Were it not for frank discussions of their initial reactions to Al-Anon or Nar-Anon meetings, as illustrated by these examples, it is doubtful that some significant others would give Al-Anon and Nar-Anon a second try. In reaching hasty conclusions, they would have lost an opportunity for bonding and for the growth and renewal that fellowship offers.

Ask such clients to try to identify what it was they had expected from Al-Anon or Nar-Anon and why they were disappointed with their initial experiences. Again, open and honest discussion can help to reduce resistance. The therapist's goal is not to challenge the client's prior experience; rather, it is to validate it and discuss it further. The therapist can be an effective problem solver once the client's current resistance is understood in its proper context.

Having acknowledged and discussed any negative sentiments toward Al-Anon or Nar-Anon, the therapist should now try to enlist the client's cooperation in giving Al-Anon or Nar-Anon (or both) a try, either for the first time or again. Clients should be reassured that this time, the therapist will be available and interested in their honest reactions to these experiences, with the goal of making them helpful.

Suggest to the client that she or he attend one or two Al-Anon or Nar-Anon meetings prior to the next session, and that she or he take a few moments to write down any reactions in her or his journal so that you can discuss it the next time you meet.

Treatment Note: Active Facilitation

If at any point in this facilitation program a client seems open to going to an Al-Anon or Nar-Anon meeting but seems anxious about doing so, it is appropriate to *actively facilitate* attendance. This is done by making a contact with an Al-Anon or Nar-Anon member who is willing to volunteer to talk to the client over the phone, to meet with them, to accompany them to a meeting, or any combination of these. This strategy can be very helpful in getting basically willing yet shy clients to attend their first meetings. It is also consistent with the 12th step of the 12-step program. An Al-Anon or Nar-Anon volunteer appropriate for this task would be someone of the same sex as the client, who has been active in Al-Anon or Nar-Anon for at least a year, who has served as an Al-Anon or Nar-Anon sponsor, and who has a sponsor of his or her own. The facilitator may locate such volunteers by networking with local Al-Anon and Nar-Anon groups.

To implement active facilitation, the therapist should contact the Al-Anon or Nar-Anon volunteer by phone, preferably with the client present, and explain that the client would like to ask a few questions, talk to a "real" Al-Anon member, or have company at a first meeting. Then, allow the client and the volunteer to talk together directly to make arrangements.

Treatment Note: Talking About the Addict

One issue that commonly arises in the course of this program, and that is best addressed from the outset, is the tendency that many codependents will have to want to talk more or less exclusively about the substance abuser. This is, of course, understandable. It is often either the explicit or implicit agenda of significant others in seeking therapy in the first place to enlist a professional's help in their efforts to get their loved ones to stop drinking or drugging. "Tell me what I can do to get him or her to stop" is the not-so-hidden agenda of many clients. As such, they may persist in wanting to talk about how to change the alcoholic or addict, whereas the facilitator's goal is to talk about how *they* (i.e., the significant others) can change.

From the Al-Anon perspective, the answer to the client's question may seem like a paradoxical and confusing one. The main tenet of Al-Anon is that the codependent needs to learn to detach from the addict's substance use: to let go of the addict, to change his or her own behavior and way of relating to the addict, and to focus on his or her own needs and development. He or she is urged to detach: to stop protecting the abuser from the natural consequences of his or her substance abuse, to stop trying to substitute his or her own willpower for that of the addict, and thereby to alter the status quo in the relationship.

Because they are not accustomed to this point of view, many significant others may persist in wanting to discuss their partners' substance use from a naive problem-solving perspective: "Tell me what I can do to get him or her to stop." Many may initially perceive the facilitator's and Al-Anon's message—in effect, that "less is more"—as unsatisfying. They may express disappointment and frustration. The therapeutic challenge is to show sympathy for the client's distress—indeed, his or her plight—while at the same time steering him or her progressively away from an enabling relationship with the addict toward caring detachment. Concretely, this means allowing the client to vent his or her frustrations yet consistently resisting any temptation to allow the session to digress to an endless discussion of the addict and what she or he is doing. This would not leave enough time for discussion of the significant other and what he or she needs to do to alter the way she or he relates to the substance abuser.

Detaching

Beginning with this session, the facilitator should end each session with one or two specific suggestions as to what the client can do to begin to decrease his or her enabling relationship with the substance abuser and move instead toward caring detachment. This process needs to be a collaborative one. As discussed earlier, detachment and enabling cannot always be rigidly defined: *This* behavior is caring detachment, *that* is enabling. What may constitute detachment in one relationship may actually seem more like enabling in another. A major factor to consider is what has been the status quo in the relationship.

The facilitator needs to begin, then, by developing a clear sense of the existing dynamics of the addict-codependent relationship. A good question to ask yourself is this: How does the codependent usually react to the substance abuser, and what kind of behavioral change in the codependent would represent a change in that dynamic? Another way to put is this: How could the client change the way she or he relates to the substance abuser so that the client is being honest, is taking better care of him or herself, and allowing the substance abuser to be more responsible?

Detachment is not an all-or-none sort of thing. There are degrees of caring detachment, and changing the addict-codependent relationship is a goal that is best approached incrementally. Positive experiences in early attempts to detach, coupled with support from the therapist and from Al-Anon or Nar-Anon, can reinforce change in the significant other. The reinforcement for change comes when the client sees that she or he is taking better care of his or her mental, physical, spiritual, or social health, or combinations of these and also, as the substance abuser reacts to these changes. It is therefore very important that the therapist point out such changes in the client's behavior, as well as the reactions of the substance abuser, as a way of supporting caring detachment.

The following case example is intended to illustrate how detaching can be approached initially.

Janet said this to her counselor in their first session: "I'm not dealing well. I'm furious on a regular basis." She was angry at her husband, Tony, an alcoholic and cocaine addict whose license had been suspended after a second DWI arrest, because she had developed a pattern of consistently giving things up that were important to her in order to take care of him. For example, she'd been scheduled for a physical exam, but when Tony asked her to drive him to a job interview, she said yes. He was late getting out from the interview, and as a result, she missed her appointment. "These things happen all the time," she complained.

In the assessment, Janet had identified Tony's stage of substance abuse, using the relational model presented earlier, as Stage Four: "He's a slave," she said, "and alcohol and drugs are his master." She also identified with the deep resentment and alienation commonly experienced by significant others at that stage. "I walk around feeling resentful all the time, and I just know that can't be good for my emotional or physical health."

As evidence to support her opinion that her husband was indeed a compulsive user, Janet cited the following facts: He had lost his license for 6 months as a result of the second DWI arrest; he had lost two consecutive jobs due to excessive absenteeism; he had stolen money from Janet and from his parents; and he had become a chronic liar. Despite these consequences, he continued to drink and get high, lamely arguing that he'd cut back. "And he lies so much to cover his tracks," Janet said, "that he's gotten in the habit of lying about things he doesn't even have to lie about."

In her relationship with Tony, Janet was not only chronically angry but terribly confused:

> I really don't know what to do. Sometimes, I think I should refuse to help him out at all, but on the other hand, I want things to get better. That's why I took him for that interview, even though I know very well that he's still using and probably wouldn't last more than a couple of weeks on the job, if he got it. Also, I don't know what to talk to him about anymore, and what not to talk about. I mean, do I vent my anger every time I feel it? If I did that, I'd be yelling at him every day. On the other hand, if I keep my lip buttoned, I just walk around steaming.

Janet's situation was not atypical of loved ones when they first seek help. They want to know what to do to change the addict, though Al-Anon teaches that what they really need help in is how to change themselves. The practitioner who uses this program will no doubt encounter Janet's sentiments and her situation time and time again. The challenge is to reassure the client that Al-Anon and the counselor have an idea of how the client's life can change for the better and how that change could influence the substance abuser in a positive way. However, that change may not be what the significant other expected.

Janet was prepared by her counselor for the reality that Tony might not welcome changes in her. In fact, the counselor said, Tony might even try to undermine any changes that Janet attempted to make in the way she related to him. "He is used to a status quo," the counselor said, "and when you change yourself and the way you relate to him, even in small ways, that will signal a change in the status quo, and you can expect a reaction."

With this in mind, Janet and the counselor jointly decided that a good place to begin the process of detachment was for Janet to do two things: (a) let Tony know that she'd started seeing a counselor because she wanted to work on how his substance abuse had affected her and (b) tell Tony that she was going to have her paycheck deposited automatically into a separate checking account in her name only. That way, he could not steal money by making withdrawals from a joint account without telling her, and she would be assured of having at least enough money to pay the essential household bills.

The counselor specifically advised Janet not to allow herself to get into arguments with Tony over these decisions or to attempt to provoke a reaction from him by presenting them in a hostile way. Instead, she was told to simply state them straight-forwardly as decisions she'd made for herself (because money had become a big stress in her life). She and the counselor role-played some potential interactions Janet might have with Tony, including him accusing her of punishing him or of trying to control him. Janet, of course, knew her husband best, and she could predict that these would in fact be likely reactions. She was right. Tony became furious and at one point stormed out of the house, only to return an hour later because he had neither money nor a vehicle.

One outcome of this case was that Tony ended up entering a treatment program about 4 months after Janet started seeing the counselor. That was a highly gratifying outcome for Janet. Just as important, however, was the fact that at the end of that time, she no longer found herself experiencing the stress of chronic resentment, and the finances were in much better shape. Through Al-Anon, she had made the first new friends she had in years. She had started a regular program of exercise and was, in general, happier than she had been, in her estimation, in two decades. She was hopeful that Tony would recover from his addictions, but she was equally determined to maintain the changes in her own lifestyle even if he didn't.

CHAPTER 9
Topic 3
Al-Anon and Nar-Anon

THE GOAL OF THIS SESSION is to extend the discussion of Al-Anon and Nar-Anon, with particular attention to their key traditions and the resources they have to offer. As with other sessions, however, it begins with a review of the client's experiences since the last session, with special emphasis on his or her reactions to recovery tasks.

▓ Review

The first 10 to 15 minutes of the session should be devoted to checking in with the client. Be sure to inquire specifically about each of the following:

Journal

Did the client start a journal? If so, are there any entries that she or he would like you to read (or read to you)? Take a few minutes to discuss any such journal entries, and encourage the client to continue journaling.

Readings

Did the client follow up on any of the suggested readings from *Alcoholics Anonymous* (AA, 1976), *Narcotics Anonymous* (NA, 1985), or *Al-Anon Faces Alcoholism* (Al-Anon, 1985)? If so, what reactions did she or he have? Were you able to give the client the NA (1983) pamphlet, *Am I an Addict?*, and if so did he or she read it?

Based on initial readings, has the client's estimation of what stage of use the substance abuser is at (from the assessment session) changed at all? If so, what stage does the significant other now believe the substance abuser is at?

Take a moment to inquire about the client's reaction to the idea, raised in the last session, of being powerless to stop a problem drinker or drug user from substance use. How does that idea sit with him or her now that there has been some time to think about it? Is he or she really accepting of it, or is there a part that resists that idea? Explain that this is an important question—one that is worthy of careful thought and discussion—because it relates directly to the first step of AA and Al-Anon. *Many loved ones of addicts secretly cling to a belief that it's possible to get an addict clean and sober, if you just try hard enough. This belief almost inevitably leads to a preoccupation with the substance abuse and to enabling.* On the other hand, if we truly accept the idea that we cannot make someone else's decisions for them—including an addict's decision about getting sober— then we are free to allow them to be responsible for themselves (including dealing with any negative consequences associated with substance abuse), which opens the way to caring detachment.

Next, introduce the idea of the client starting to shift attention away from the addict, toward his or her own needs. This shifting of focus also facilitates caring detachment. It is an idea that is much easier to act on if one first accepts the notion of being unable to change anyone other than ourselves—of being able to make decisions only for ourselves. The story titled, "The Face of an Angel," in *Al-Anon Faces Alcoholism* (Al-Anon, 1985), expresses this idea in a clear and poignant way. The therapist can ask the significant other if she or he has read this story; if not, the therapist may want to summarize it and then discuss the basic idea of detaching that this story so aptly presents.

Meetings

Inquire next about any reactions to Al-Anon or Nar-Anon meetings that the client may have attended. Because these may be a significant other's first exposure to 12-step fellowships, take some extra time in this session to elicit and explore reactions to these first meetings, with special attention to resolving issues that might undermine motivation to continue going. Common forms of resistance include resisting identifying with other members, discomfort with spirituality, social shyness, and last but not least, saying: "I'm not as bad off as those people!" This last form of resistance can be handled by pointing out that Al-Anon and Nar-Anon can be as helpful for concerned others of those with more moderate substance abuse problems as they are for concerned others of those with severe addictions.

Detaching

Did the client make any initial efforts at practicing caring detachment? If so, what did he or she do? Does what he or she say strike the therapist as caring detachment? Especially in these early sessions, it is important not only to encourage and reinforce caring detachment but also to be sure that the significant other understands the concept and is acting consistently with it in relation to the substance abuser. Consider the following example of one client who confused detaching with *accommodating.*

Julie had lived with her boyfriend Jake for 3 years. She first noticed that he had a drinking problem after they moved in together. She'd always known that he liked to drink, but while they were dating, she didn't realize that he drank not only when they went out but all the time. Weekdays, he'd often start off with a beer in the morning before going to work and then stop at a bar for two or three more on the way home. He admitted to Julie that the only reason he didn't drink on the job was that he worked in construction and would have been fired on the spot if his supervisor caught him with a beer. Evenings and weekends, he drank more or less continuously. He was rarely farther than an arm's length from a beer.

Although they'd fought occasionally about paying bills (Jake, spending too much in the bar, often came up short when it was time to pay his share of the household expenses), so far, the negative consequences associated with his drinking had been largely interpersonal: Julie's feelings for Jake had started to change. As she put it, she still loved him, but she was definitely no longer as attracted to him as she once had been. She felt that this change in her was directly related to how she felt about his drinking. In turn, it was beginning to cause trouble between them. For example, Julie found that she did not want to make love with Jake anymore when he smelled of beer. And day-to-day life had become quite boring for her, with him usually falling asleep on the couch by 9:00 at night.

In time, Julie found herself making little sarcastic comments about Jake's drinking, particularly about his after-work "shopping trips" to the bar and his early bedtime. He acted like he didn't hear these comments. In time, she started making more pointed remarks. To these, he responded with irritation, calling Julie "Mother." So far, she'd avoided confronting Jake with her most serious concern about his drinking, though, which had to do with her changing feelings toward him.

Julie decided to get some counseling for herself after this last bridge had been crossed. It had been her most difficult interaction with Jake to date. He had approached her for sex one night, and she'd said something about his being too drunk. He exploded. He stormed out of their apartment and did not show up until the next evening, refusing to tell Julie where he'd been. In response to his demands, she found herself apologizing, though only halfheartedly, and internally, it bothered her a great deal to do so.

After meeting twice with a counselor, Julie thought she understood what detaching was all about. At the start of her third session, she said that things were much better between her and Jake. The counselor asked why—what had changed? Julie explained that she'd decided to stop talking to Jake about his drinking and, in her words, "To just see where things go between us." The counselor was puzzled. She asked Julie if that meant that Jake's drinking didn't bother her anymore. Julie shook her head. "Oh, it still bothers me, all right, but there's nothing I can do about it, right? So I'm, you know, detaching myself from it."

The counselor replied,

> To tell you the truth, what you're describing sounds to me more like enabling than detaching. You're giving Jake a signal that the status quo in your relationship is fine when it isn't. From my point of view, you started to detach that night you told him the truth about how his drinking affects your sexual desire. That was a signal that things were not OK. Actually, you were taking care of yourself by being honest and not compromising your sexuality. You weren't just complaining—you were confronting him with a reality. You were also allowing Jake to experience the natural—and perfectly understandable—consequences of his drinking, which is your loss of attraction.

This discussion proved to be very productive. Julie began to be honest again with Jake. She extended this beyond her sexual feelings and told him about how she was bored with the rut their life was in. She started making dates to see old friends she'd fallen out of touch with, and she also started going to Al-Anon. The tension in her relationship with Jake did increase, but he also started drinking less. A few months later, she told him that she was no longer sure that she wanted to commit to Jake and had decided they should live apart. At that point, he said he would go for help about his drinking. Julie replied that that was probably a good idea for Jake. "I told him I really hope it works out for him because I care about him, and I think that eventually, drinking the way he does will kill him." She told him she still had some hope that their relationship would work out. "But for now," she said, "I told him I'd prefer to be on my own."

New Material

In this session, the therapist should endeavor to engage the significant other in a discussion of some of the key traditions that guide the fellowships of Al-Anon and Nar-Anon and also to help the significant other identify some of the resources that Al-Anon and Nar-Anon have to offer in support of his or her own recovery.

Traditions

Community

To begin this discussion of Al-Anon and Nar-Anon traditions, point out that the 12 steps all use the word *we* instead of *I*. This is because all 12-step fellowships are founded on the belief that group support is superior to individual willpower when it comes to stopping alcohol or drug abuse. Al-Anon and Nar-Anon believe that individuals who have loved ones who have substance use problems can effectively learn to cope with those substance use problems by opening themselves up and availing themselves of that mutual support. Beyond that, Al-Anon and Nar-Anon are based on the belief that the addict is more likely to pursue recovery when his or her loved ones stop enabling the substance abuse problem. Here is an example:

Lisa had been married to Jeff for 5 years. They had two young children, ages 4 and 2. Jeff was a habitual drinker and a frequent user of cocaine, and his habits were creating a major financial crisis for the family. Lisa saw a counselor who urged her to begin attending Al-Anon or Nar-Anon meetings in her area. She found the former more accessible and also felt more comfortable in them because her own father had been an alcoholic. She learned, both through counseling and those first Al-Anon meetings, that she had been enabling Jeff's use by taking responsibility for managing their increasingly difficult finances. She concluded that this approach was only forestalling disaster. She began to detach first by speaking up about their financial problems. She had hesitated to do so only because she'd felt it would make no difference. "If it gets a reaction," one woman at a meeting said, "then that's a difference. You take that and you go from there." Her counselor agreed, adding only the caveat that Lisa was better off bringing these things up when Jeff was sober.

Lisa had never been an assertive type and so she needed a lot of support from the other members of Al-Anon to experiment with changes in the way she related to Jeff.

He sensed this and began to complain about her going to meetings, saying it sounded like "a bunch of man haters." But Lisa persisted. Next, she spoke to Jeff about her concerns about him as a role model for their children, especially in light of her experiences with her alcoholic father. She felt that her remote and unsatisfying relationship with her father was a major reason why she'd grown up with poor self-esteem.

A crisis point in the marriage came when Lisa, who like Jeff worked full time and actually made more money than he did, refused to give him $50 when he asked for it, saying she needed the money for bills. Jeff took her purse, emptied the contents onto the floor, and then took all the cash from her wallet. That night, Lisa shared this incident at an Al-Anon meeting. Over the next several days, she received calls daily from at least two other members offering support and asking her how she was doing. This made a big difference for Lisa, who told her counselor she probably could not have done what she was doing if it weren't for the support she was getting from her Al-Anon friends. She knew that she needed to have the courage to persevere, and she knew that the community of Al-Anon would there for her.

◆

Ask the client to share his or her reactions to this idea that fellowship and group support can be superior to going it alone when learning to detach from another person's substance use problem. Questions such as the following can help to facilitate this discussion:

Have you ever felt all alone in your struggle to deal with _____ 's substance abuse problem?

Have you ever felt overwhelmed, helpless, or hopeless in the face of _____ 's substance abuse problem?

Have you hesitated to reach out to others for support and guidance in dealing with _____ 's substance use problem? If so, why?

Have you been afraid to express your true feelings to _____ about his or her substance use? Why?

Spirituality

Spirituality is another strong tradition within 12-step fellowships. Al-Anon and Nar-Anon, like AA and NA, espouse faith in a Higher Power. Many individuals misinterpret this as a statement of religious orthodoxy, when in fact, it is not that at all. Rather, the approach to faith advocated by 12-step fellowships has been described as follows:

Faith [in the 12-step sense] refers to the personal actions and responses involved in *awakening* to meanings and values, and in committing the self to centers of value, images, and reality of power, and core stories that link persons to others who share them. (Fowler, 1993, p. 116)

It is in the foregoing sense that AA and NA call themselves programs of spiritual renewal. Bill Wilson, for example, described AA as a fellowship that was founded on the idea that an excessive belief in personal willpower constitutes an ultimately self-destructive core story by which to live. He wrote,

The *first requirement* is that we be convinced that any life run on self-will can hardly be a success. . . . Most people try to live by self-propulsion. Each person is like an actor who wants to run the whole show; is forever trying to arrange the lights, the ballet, the scenery and the rest of the players in his own way. If his arrangements would stay put, if only people would do as he wished, the show would be great. (AA, 1976, p. 60)

This is one way of saying that a culture that embraces a social philosophy of radical individualism, and which thereby promotes self-reliance to an extreme, is spiritually dysfunctional. No one can truly be such an island unto themselves. As a society, we set ourselves up for personal and relational dysfunction on a massive scale when we create a cult of self-reliance. Conversely, it has been argued that there is power to be derived from acknowledging personal limitation (Bill W., 1992). That power has its roots in humility and willingness to trust the collective wisdom of a group of concerned individuals and follow its advice.

The spirituality of 12-step fellowships is based on the concept of group bonding and collective wisdom being superior to radical individualism as an approach to life. They seek collective strength through humbly accepting individual limitation. They have a set of shared values as expressed in the 12 steps, in the Serenity Prayer,[1] and in their traditions. They seek to foster interpersonal connectedness and reliance on group support and on wisdom passed down, as opposed to self-will run riot. They seek to promote growth and renewal through advocacy of a core story that challenges the idea that we are all islands unto ourselves, and that emphasizes instead acceptance of personal limitation and surrender to a power greater than personal ego.

This brief overview is intended to clarify the difference between a *fellowship* that is guided by what could be called a spiritual philosophy and a rich oral history and an *organized religion,* which neither AA nor Al-Anon (nor any other 12-step fellowship) are. There is no priesthood, secular or otherwise, to be found in 12-step fellowships. There is only the most loosely organized central organization, which bears no responsibility for issuing, monitoring, or correcting dogma.

This is very important for the significant other to understand: *Twelve-step fellowships advocate an approach to life and a system of values but not a particular concept of God, much less a religious dogma.*

Even if the client has not expressed concerns or reservations about religiosity and its place in Al-Anon or Nar-Anon, the therapist is wise to raise this issue anyway. Ask the client if she or he experiences any discomfort about the idea of a Higher Power as it is used in 12-step fellowships and if so, why. Listen carefully to any concerns or objections and then try to clarify them in light of the preceding information. Point out that the client is not likely to encounter protracted discussions of religion at Al-Anon or Nar-Anon meetings, though there may be some talk about spirituality. In Al-Anon and Nar-Anon, individuals are free to interpret the concept of a Higher Power in any way they choose, so long as they acknowledge some power or force greater and wiser than sheer individual willpower.

Fellowship With Alcoholics Anonymous

Al-Anon and Nar-Anon, by tradition, stand as fellowships of peers that are independent of Alcoholics Anonymous and Narcotics Anonymous but that nevertheless remain committed to AA and NA and the 12-step program as an effective way for individuals to overcome problems with alcohol or drugs. Significant others should be made aware of the faith that Al-Anon and Nar-Anon place in AA and NA. Rather than trying to reform or cure a partner's substance use problem, Al-Anon and Nar-Anon members encourage one another to detach. If and when the substance abuser wants help in stopping drinking or using, he or she can be referred to the resources of AA or NA or both. It is not the significant other's responsibility to monitor, much less coordinate, the substance abuser's recovery.

The therapist should check to see that the client understands this concept of fellowship with AA and NA and how 12-step fellowships work together based on common values and ideas about the nature of addiction and recovery.

Resources: How Al-Anon and Nar-Anon Help

The point has been made that to the uninitiated, Al-Anon and Nar-Anon (like AA and NA) are often mistaken for religious organizations. In reality, they are fellowships (or extended families of sorts) that provide an array of resources for the support and welfare of their members. The therapist should reiterate this point and take some time to describe the following resources that Al-Anon and Nar-Anon have to offer.

Information Services

Telephone numbers for Al-Anon and Nar-Anon information services can be found in many local telephone books. These numbers are listed in the white pages under "Al-Anon (or Nar-Anon) Family Groups." If Al-Anon or Nar-Anon are not listed, individuals can try calling InfoLine or similar public information services. These services will often have current meeting schedules.

Services such as InfoLine, as well as AA and Al-Anon hot lines, are often available 24 hours a day, 365 days a year. They can refer a significant other (or a substance abuser) to the nearest and soonest meeting in their areas. They can also offer crisis counseling (by nonprofessionals) to callers who have acute needs for support or advice or both. Such advice will always be consistent with 12-step philosophy and will, in general, be simple and practical. Most often, the caller will be urged to get to a meeting as soon as possible to get face-to-face support in dealing with his or her situation.

Treatment Note: Making Calls for Substance Abusers

The therapist may want to let the client know that the substance abuser can also make use of these referral services if and when they are ready to seek help for his or her alcohol or drug problem. The client may want to make this information available to the substance abuser; however, the significant other should *not* be the one to get information (i.e., make the calls) for the substance abuser, because to do so would only serve to reinforce the idea that the client is responsible for the substance abuser's recovery. From the outset, it is the substance abuser who should take responsibility (and therefore get the credit) for his or her decision to pursue recovery.

Meetings

Meetings, of course, are the heart of all 12-step fellowships. Al-Anon and Nar-Anon are self-supporting fellowships that charge no user fees. Significant others should be aware that anyone attending an Al-Anon or Nar-Anon meeting may contribute a small amount to pay for items such as coffee or publications that the group lends to members. However, there is no obligation to contribute any money; therefore, lack of money represents no barrier to taking advantage of Al-Anon or Nar-Anon.

Meetings are open to anyone who has a family member or loved one who has an alcohol or drug problem. The focus of meetings, however, is often at least as much on the welfare and growth of those who are there as it is on the addicts they are in relationships with. Initially, this focus on the loved ones of substance abusers instead of on the substance abusers may frustrate or disappoint the newcomer, especially one who is feeling desperate and seeks an immediate solution to how to get the drinker or drug user to stop. Sometimes, codependents go to their first meetings hoping to hear something they had not yet thought of. In time, it is hoped, they come to see the usefulness of focusing on their own growth and on changing the basic structure and dynamics of their relationships with the substance abusers as the wiser path than trying to substitute their own willpower and motivation for the addicts' or trying to control the substance users through some single act or intervention on their parts.

Meetings offer social contact and friendship, a supportive environment in which to vent emotions, practical advice on handling difficult situations, suggestions for how to detach from instead of enabling the addict, and in general, the opportunity to learn from others' stories of recovery. One of the keys to Al-Anon and Nar-Anon's effectiveness lies in the abilities of members to identify with and learn from each others' experiences and to support each others' efforts to change their relationships with the substance abusers.

The therapist might want to take a few moments here to solicit questions about meetings and provide additional information about them if the client does have any. To the extent that the therapist is personally familiar with any Al-Anon or Nar-Anon meetings, she or he can share information that might encourage the reluctant client to get to his or her first meeting.

Publications

Al-Anon and Nar-Anon publish a number of books and pamphlets, including the book, *Al-Anon Faces Alcoholism* (Al-Anon, 1985), that is used as a basic text in this treatment program. Books and pamphlets, which are often available through group meetings, not only explain Al-Anon and Nar-Anon concepts but also can augment and help to clarify what the client hears at meetings. Clients should be encouraged to use Al-Anon and Nar-Anon publications in this way, as they serve as a source of comfort and advice between meetings.

Telephone Therapy

The facilitator should advise clients in advance that they are likely to find people asking for their phone numbers, and also offering to give out their phone numbers in return, at Al-Anon and Nar-Anon meetings. To some newcomers—especially those who are socially shy or ambivalent about Al-Anon or Nar-Anon—this can be a discomforting experience at first. Some individuals misinterpret these efforts to reach out as an effort to establish a level of intimacy they are uncomfortable with.

Explain to clients that people like themselves have found that as addiction progresses, many significant others find themselves becoming increasingly isolated from their own support networks of family and friends. In part, this may be a consequence of wanting to avoid the shame and stigma that they fear would result if their loved ones' substance problems became known. In time, this social avoidance and secrecy can evolve into a *wall of silence* that surrounds the significant other. Breaking through this wall—for instance, by opening oneself to contact with other Al-Anon or Nar-Anon members—can be no easy task, especially if the isolation has been long-standing. Therapists often find themselves working very hard with the loved ones of addicts on this basic issue of becoming open to support and contact. It is, however, worth the effort.

Explain to the client that the use of telephone therapy is a long-standing tradition and a vital part of the 12-step recovery culture. Al-Anon, Nar-Anon, AA, and NA members are all encouraged to call other members for support not only in times of crisis but also to relieve the sense of isolation and chronic frustration that many of them must live with day to day. To use the telephone effectively, one must first learn to overcome any "telephone phobia" (i.e., social anxiety) that may stand in the way.

Aside from breaking through the social isolation that many loved ones of substance abusers experience, telephone therapy has a practical purpose that has to do with anticipating crises. One therapist who used this program, when discussing telephone therapy, would routinely ask the following question: "When you're in a jam, who would you rather call: a stranger or a friend?" The answer is obvious. Significant others need to develop a network of Al-Anon or Nar-Anon friends *in advance of a crisis* to feel comfortable using that network if and when a crisis does occur. This is an important reason for getting and using other members' phone numbers and in general for getting to know others through meetings.

Sponsors

Although more will be said about sponsors in later sessions in this program, the therapist should at least briefly discuss this important resource in the present context of introducing the client to Al-Anon and Nar-Anon.

Ask the client if she or he has heard this term and if so, what his or her idea of a sponsor is. Check to see that the client is aware of these basic points: A sponsor is an active member of Al-Anon or Nar-Anon who takes on a responsibility something like that of a coach. A sponsor is chosen voluntarily and should be of the same sex as the client. A sponsor should have been active in Al-Anon or Nar-Anon for at least 2 years and should have a sponsor of his or her own.

For the newcomer, a sponsor is a source of information about Al-Anon or Nar-Anon and about "working" the 12-step program in addition to being an important source of comfort, support, and advice. A sponsor is not a therapist or a marriage counselor, however; nor should a sponsor be thought of as someone who has the last word on any issue. Sponsors can be changed at any time and probably should be changed once in a while.

Newcomers can benefit a great deal from establishing a relationship with a temporary sponsor for their first 6 months in the fellowship. Regular one-to-one contact with a sponsor affords an opportunity to ask questions and to share feelings that the newcomer might be reticent to ask or share in a group. Many misconceptions about the 12-step program and about Al-Anon or Nar-Anon can be corrected through the sponsor-newcomer relationship, and the process of bonding to the fellowship can also begin through this relationship.

To get a sponsor, a newcomer needs only to state at the start of one or more meetings that she or he is looking for a temporary sponsor. Members who qualify and who feel ready to take on this role will identify themselves. It is advisable that the newcomer talk with the potential sponsor (and preferably two or more potential sponsors) several times before reaching a mutual agreement to establish a sponsor-sponsee relationship.

▒ Summing Up

Before moving on to recovery tasks, take a moment to ask the client to share what she or he got out of this session. What did she or he learn? What, if anything, was valuable about this session? Does she or he have any questions about the things that were discussed?

As a general rule, it is recommended that therapists take a couple of minutes to sum up at the end of each session, before suggesting any recovery tasks. Simply repeat the two or three points that you especially want the client to have gotten out of this session, and check to see that those points have gotten across.

▒ Recovery Tasks

Suggested recovery tasks to follow up on this topic are as follows:

Meetings

The therapist should again make a specific suggestion that the client attend two Al-Anon or Nar-Anon meetings before the next session. Again, it is advisable to have on hand current Al-Anon and Nar-Anon meeting schedules for use in locating meetings that would be convenient in terms of time and location.

If the client has not yet gone to any meetings but now expresses a willingness to do so, identify two meetings that would be convenient. Remind the client to identify himself or herself as a newcomer and to focus primarily on listening at these initial meetings. She or he should listen with the goal of trying to identify with at least some of what is said. Also, encourage the client to comment on these first experiences at meetings in his or her journal.

The newcomer needs to be made aware that they are likely to find that meetings are different from one another. Explain that this is one reason why you are suggesting that they attend two different meetings. Also, advise them that they may not relate to everyone at a meeting but that if they listen with an open mind, they may well be able to identify with at least some aspects of many members' experiences.

Treatment Note: Approaching Resistance

When dealing with reluctant or skeptical clients, one initial strategy is to frame this recovery task as asking them to give Al-Anon or Nar-Anon a fair try and to approach meetings with an open mind. Indicate that you will be very interested in hearing about their reactions to meetings and to help them sort out what is useful from what is not as they continue to work with you.

Treatment Note: Shyness

For the shy or anxious client, the therapist can consider using active facilitation in getting him or her to first meetings. Active facilitation is described at the end of Topic 2.

Readings

Suggest to the client that they read the following between sessions, to extend the benefits of this discussion:

Al-Anon Faces Alcoholism (Al-Anon, 1985) pages 231-240: "The Nature of the Fellowship" and "The 12 Steps and 12 Traditions"

Al-Anon (1979) pamphlet, *Understanding Ourselves and Alcoholism*

Journal

If the client has been maintaining a journal, remind him or her to write down any thoughts or reactions she or he may have to readings, meetings, or to these facilitation sessions, for future discussion.

Detaching

Suggest one or two specific things the client can do to begin to decrease his or her enabling relationship with the substance abuser and to relate to him or her increasingly via caring detachment. As always, this recovery task should be approached as a collaborative task. Its success depends in large part on the therapist developing a good conceptual understanding of caring detachment, an understanding of the dynamics of the addict-codependent relationship, and an appreciation of the need for most significant others to detach gradually (i.e., to change their relationships to the addicts incrementally as opposed to abruptly).

Note

1. "God grant me the serenity to accept the things I cannot change, the courage to change the things I can, and the wisdom to know the difference."

CHAPTER 10

Topic 4
Denial

I N THIS SESSION, the therapist presents and discusses the dynamic process of denial as it pertains to both addicts and codependents. *Denial is a common psychological defense against loss of control.* Denial can be reflected in inconsistencies between one's words and one's actions and in discrepancies between how individuals view themselves versus how they are viewed by others. Although it is a common and understandable reaction to loss of control, denial must be worked through for the substance abuser as well as the significant other to begin their respective recovery processes. This is accomplished in part through educating the addict (or the significant other) about denial and in part through consistently pointing out discrepancies between his or her words versus his or her actions or self-views in comparison to others' perceptions of them.

▨ Review

Once more, begin the session by devoting the first 10 minutes or so to check in (i.e., discussing the client's experiences since the last session). Ask whether the client has made any journal entries that he or she would like to share. Then, be sure to touch base in each of the following areas:

Meetings

How many Al-Anon or Nar-Anon meetings did the client attend? Was she or he comfortable there? If not, why?

What thoughts or emotional reactions did the client have to meetings? Are there any questions about meetings that the therapist can help to answer?

Does the client have any reservations about continuing to attend Al-Anon or Nar-Anon meetings? Ask him or her, "What can you potentially gain from continued participation in Al-Anon or Nar-Anon?"

Readings

Did the client follow up on the suggested readings? Did she or he read the Al-Anon (1979) pamphlet, *Understanding Ourselves and Alcoholism*? Did she or he have any reactions to it?

Detaching

What, if any, actions did the client take since the last session to start or continue the process of caring detachment? What was his or her level of comfort in doing this? What, if any, reaction was there from the substance abuser? Is there anything the therapist can help to clarify with respect to detaching?

New Material

Begin by reading one or more of the following passages:

Our drinking careers have been characterized by countless vain attempts to prove we could drink like other people. The idea that somehow, someday he will control and enjoy his drinking is the great obsession of every abnormal drinker. (AA, 1976, p. 30)

We have seen the truth demonstrated again and again: "Once an alcoholic, always an alcoholic." Commencing to drink after a period of sobriety, we are in a short time as bad as ever. (AA, 1976, p. 33)

Many of us tried to stop using on sheer willpower. This action was a temporary solution. We saw that willpower alone would not work for any length of time. (NA, 1987, p. 20)

The above quotes from *Alcoholics Anonymous* (1976) and *Narcotics Anonymous* (1987) capture the essence of the concept of denial. The alcoholic or addict who is in denial lives with the illusion that she or he can somehow control or limit substance use or use some psychoactive substances "safely". The addict stubbornly refuses to accept the reality of psychological or physical dependence or both.

The lives of alcoholics and drug addicts are typically marked by brief periods of abstinence and countless attempts to limit use. Despite failure after failure on the part of alcoholics or addicts to drink or use like "normal" (i.e., nonaddicted) people, they continue to try to convince themselves (and usually others as well) that they (and not alcohol or drugs) are in control. Following a period of abstinence, the addict begins substance use again, often with every good intention of limiting use, only to find that in short order they are "as bad as ever," as Bill Wilson put it. Subjectively, denial could be described as the refusal to accept this limitation of personal willpower; objectively, it is the inability to effectively control substance use.

Just as addicts can engage in denial, so can their significant others. Denial has its parallels, in other words, in both substance abusers and their significant others. One spouse of an addict described the situation within a family dealing with addiction this way: "The family denies a [substance use] problem exists at all and excuses it as 'going through a stage,' 'a terrible boss,' or 'too many pressures' to account for the excess [substance use]" (Mary M., 1985, p. 4).

Aside from seeking an excuse to justify substance abuse, as in the preceding quote, a significant other may acknowledge that a substance use problem exists but resist the idea that he or she is essentially powerless to make the drinker or user stop. Both of these forms of denial are common among significant others of substance abusers and are the focus of discussion here.

Denial in the Addict

The therapist can use the following material as the basis for a discussion of denial as it applies to alcoholics and drug addicts. This will be followed by a discussion of how the concept of denial applies to significant others.

Denial is the term used to refer to the emotional and intellectual difficulties—in a word, the internal resistance—people typically experience when confronted with personal limitations or losses. As stated earlier, this resistance tends to be greater in a society, such as ours, which has a strong tradition of believing in virtually limitless self-determination. Men and women in our culture react more negatively to the notion of personal limitation and powerlessness than would those whose cultures are more accepting of personal limitation.

With respect to alcoholism and addiction, the roots of denial lie in how it feels to be faced with loss of control—in this case, over substance use—as well as the necessity to give it up for good. This is what Step 1 of the 12 steps (acceptance) is about.

Confronting the personal limitation posed by dependency on alcohol or drugs can cause discomfort in anyone, to be sure. In our society, the idea of powerlessness tends to arouse intense feelings of anxiety, anger, shame, inadequacy, and guilt. Powerlessness can pose a decided threat to self-esteem, as the following exchange between a counselor and a young alcoholic in early treatment reveals.

Anthony was asked by his counselor to tell her how he felt if he thought about being powerless over alcohol.

"Not very good," Anthony replied. "It makes me feel less confident."

"Tell me more about that," the counselor said.

"It makes me feel like I've failed," said Anthony.

"Failed how?" asked the counselor.

"Like I'm not strong willed, not strong-minded enough," Anthony replied.

"And you don't like that idea?" asked the counselor.

"It's definitely not the way I want to think of myself," said Anthony. "And it's not the way I want to be looked at by others."

This interaction as well as the following case example can be used as vehicles for illustrating some of the points made later on. The therapist should feel free to use alternative means of illustrating these concepts—for example, through other case examples, stories from the AA or NA big books, and so forth. However it is done, *it is very important that the concept of denial and its various forms be illustrated via some concrete examples and not merely presented in abstract terms.*

Bob attempted to avoid coming to terms with his loss of control over substance use as fiercely as any alcoholic might. His first line of defense was to get angry whenever the subject was brought up by anyone else, such as his wife or one of his children. After blowing up, he'd usually change the subject, either launching into an attack on the other person or else complaining long and loudly about some other problem, such as finances or his annoying in-laws. In response to the ever-growing list of household chores that went undone, he pleaded fatigue—after all, he said, he worked hard all week and needed the weekends to unwind.

Not surprisingly, Bob's denial extended outwardly to his behavior and inwardly to his own thought processes. For example, he went out of his way to associate with men who drank as much or even more than he did and then comforted himself by drawing the comparison between his own use and theirs. Of course, he concluded that he was merely "average" (and therefore "normal") as compared to his peers. At times, when he felt guilty pouring a fifth or sixth martini, he'd tell himself that he "deserved" it, for example, because of the stress of having to endure an unsatisfying job. His trouble at work he wrote off to a combination of bad luck and a mean-spirited, overly ambitious boss. His initial experiences of sexual impotence he attributed to his wife's rejection of him and her preoccupation with the children. And so on.

In these and other ways, Bob was able to fend off the complaints of others as well as his own nagging conscience; meanwhile, the quality of his life and his own health steadily declined. It was only when he faced disciplinary action at work, a wife who was talking about separation, chronic sexual impotence, and early symptoms of diabetes that Bob reluctantly took his first hard look at his drinking and his ability to control it.

Discussing Powerlessness

Ask the client how it might feel to be powerless over alcohol or drugs. Help him or her to articulate both emotional and intellectual reactions to the notion of powerlessness by using open-ended questions such as the following:

How do you think Bob (or Anthony), in the preceding examples, felt about the idea of their being powerless over substance use?

How do you think your own loved one feels, emotionally speaking, about the idea of being powerless to control his or her drinking or drug use?

Have you personally ever felt powerless over something in your life? What were you powerless over, and how did that feel?

What do you think it would be like to feel that you were losing control of (i.e., becoming powerless over) substance use?

Following this dialogue, go on to explain and illustrate the following forms of denial:

Simple Denial

It is normal for people to protect themselves from the psychological pain that results from limitation or loss. One of the easiest ways to do this is to deny the reality of the limitation or loss. Simple denial amounts to refusing to face facts: refusing to make the connection between one's own behavior and its consequences or refusing to face up to increasing unmanageability, loss of control over substance use, and physical and psychological dependence. Examples of simple denial of a substance use problem include the following:

Refusing to discuss substance use, period

Refusing to accurately attribute obvious consequences of substance use: attributing a driving accident to slippery roads or bad tires rather than to driving while intoxicated, attributing trouble on the job to a mean supervisor rather than to daily drug or alcohol abuse, and so on

Rejecting clear evidence of one's own failures to stop or limit substance use

Minimizing and Maximizing

In this form of denial, the individual minimizes his or her own substance use and its consequences by drawing false comparisons between his or her use and that of others. Here are some examples:

Understating the negative consequences of substance use to oneself while simultaneously exaggerating the consequences of others' substance use (e.g., "I spend less than $100 a week on cocaine; Jeff spends that much every day.")

Accusing others of exaggerating one's own use and its negative consequences (e.g., "I'm not as bad as you're making me out to be.")

Grossly overstating others' level of substance use to normalize one's own (e.g., "Joe gets high every day at work, but I just use in the evening.")

Avoidance

Sometimes, alcoholics and addicts avoid coming to terms with their substance use problems by minimizing contact with family members or others who might observe and confront them. In doing so, they try to keep the extent of their relationships with alcohol or drugs secret. For example, an alcoholic may spend much of his free time at a local "club." He may consistently come home drunk, but no one is there to witness just how much he drank at the club. And more than one alcoholic has spent virtually every evening holed up in some basement workshop, puttering around and drinking until everyone else has gone to bed. The wife of one such man sensed clearly that her husband was really married to the booze, but he insisted was that he was just pursuing his hobby.

Rationalizing

This form of denial involves finding excuses for substance use. Some of the more common justifications include the following:

Work, family, or marital stress

Depression or anxiety

Physical pain, discomfort, or insomnia

Social pressure ("Everyone else was drinking.")

Distracting

Another way to avoid having to come to terms with one's loss of control over substance use is to distract others anytime the issue comes up by simply changing the subject. Alcoholics and addicts can be remarkably clever at this. A wife may begin a conversation with every intention of talking to her husband about some negative consequence that seems clearly associated with his drinking only to find herself lured into a discussion of their marital problems, his frustrations at work, or problems with their children.

A particularly clever version of this tactic is to redirect the discussion from the addict to the significant other. Many a loved one of a substance abuser has found themselves on the defensive, talking about some problem of his or her own, every time he or she tries to confront the substance abuser.

Pseudochoice

In this form of denial, the individual acknowledges excessive substance use or negative consequences of substance use, or both, but then attempts to attribute both use and its consequences to choice rather than to progressive loss of control. A gregarious alcoholic may, for instance, attribute his tendency to get falling-down drunk four or five times a week to his "party personality," thereby implying that the behavior is voluntary (and therefore, under control). Or a stressed-out cocaine abuser may acknowledge getting into trouble at work or with the law but then explain away these consequences of substance use as reflections of his "rebellious personality." Again, the implication is that the user is choosing to use cocaine and to act rebelliously. This maneuver attempts to avoid the alternative attribution: that loss of control over cocaine use is responsible for the consequences.

Bargaining

One of the most common forms of denial, bargaining is agreeing to limit or control either the amount or type of alcohol or drugs used or when they are used as opposed to abstaining from use. Bargaining can be thought of as placating—either one's own conscience or the expressed concerns of others. One substance abuser, for example, told his wife that he would only use cocaine on special occasions. Initially, this meant holidays, but soon, the list of special occasions became very long indeed!

Other typical examples of bargaining include swearing off some kinds of substances (but not others) or some forms of them (e.g., hard liquor) as opposed to others (wine or beer) or some routes of administration (e.g., snorting vs. injecting heroin).

Behavioral Correlates of Denial

Denial, as a means of resisting acceptance of progressive loss of control over drug or alcohol use, can take on various forms as described earlier. These forms of denial concern mainly what the substance abuser *says* (or doesn't say). Denial can also be identified through close observation of the substance abuser's *behavior*, in other words, with the way she or he acts. It is useful to educate significant others about this so as to support their own beliefs about the substance abusers' drinking or drug problems in the face of denial.

Significant others of substance abusers can expect to encounter stiff resistance to the suggestion that someone is in fact addicted. Clever and persistent denial on the part of the addict can inject an element of doubt in the minds of many loved ones. To counter this, and to be able to have confidence in their own perceptions (as opposed to what the substance abusers say), significant others can be taught to recognize other behavioral signs of denial. Therapists, of course, can also use this information when dealing with a resistant addict or substance abuser.

Self-Perception Versus Perceptions of Others

The first way in which denial becomes evident on a behavioral level is through the discrepancy between the way substance abusers view themselves versus how they are viewed by others. Here is an example:

Victor, a successful professional, had been drinking virtually daily for 15 years. For almost as long, he'd also been smoking marijuana once or twice during the week and virtually every day on the weekend. His wife, Mary, sought help because she was feeling depressed and frustrated. No matter how much she complained to him, he staunchly refused to consider even moderating, much less stopping, either his marijuana use or his drinking. With respect to the former, he insisted that the children did not know he smoked pot because he was discreet about it. Mary wasn't so sure.

Of primary concern to Mary was the fact that their two sons were getting to an age where she felt they definitely suspected the truth about their father. They had, for instance, already asked probing questions to her about his drug history. She was concerned not only for how it might affect their respect for their father if it were confirmed that he was a pot head or an alcoholic but was also worried about the message that that would communicate to them: that drinking and smoking marijuana was OK.

Victor agreed with great reluctance to see a counselor with Mary. In defending his marijuana use, he had this to say:

> It relaxes me. I've always been an intense, distractible person by nature. I'm something of a workaholic. Mary's known that since she's known me. And for years, my smoking was OK with her. She even did some herself, way back when. Smoking a joint or two relaxes me. It actually makes me feel more focused.

Asked if she agreed with Victor's self-assessment, Mary shook her head. "No," she said, "that's not the way I experience Victor when he's high. And it's not the way the kids experience him, either. They're getting older now, and they're starting to ask me questions—like, "Why is Dad so out of it?""

Mary was encouraged by the therapist to go to Al-Anon meetings and also to stick with her perception that smoking pot definitely affected Victor's behavior in ways that, as she put it, "Makes him a nonentity in the family. It's like I don't really have a husband and the boys don't have a father, whenever he's high, but especially on the weekends." She was further encouraged to consider starting to do things with their sons without Victor on weekends if he chose to get high.

In this example, Victor's self-perception—that he was more relaxed and focused on marijuana—was inconsistent with the way his wife and children viewed his behavior. Although she'd had this perception before, without the validation and support of a third party (the therapist), Mary had backed down in the face of Victor's adamant insistence that pot did not affect him. With that support, she was able to take her first steps toward relating to Victor in a different way and thereby begin a process of recovery that eventually led to Victor becoming clean and sober.

Words Versus Actions

Another way in which denial is manifested has to do with discrepancies between what the substance abuser says about his or her substance use, versus what she or her does. Here is another example:

Doug had been through treatment twice before for alcoholism and after his last relapse, his wife was close to divorcing him. He told his new counselor, "This time, I finally admit it—I am powerless over alcohol. I have to give it up. No more playing around with ideas of social drinking for me. I know now that I can't drink at all."

These remarks were made in the context of a couples session with Doug and his wife, June, and judging by what he said, it appeared that Doug was highly motivated to stop drinking. To further support this statement of acceptance of the first step of AA, Doug said that he was attending three to four AA meetings a week, had been reading the Big Book, and had approached someone to be his sponsor.

All of the behaviors that Doug cited—and that June could confirm were true— could be said to be consistent with Doug's words. He said he was powerless over alcohol, and he was acting in ways consistent with such a belief. However, as this session went on, the therapist also learned that Doug was still seeing some of his old drinking buddies on a regular basis; moreover, he had even met with them at bars! When questioned about the apparent inconsistency between admitting powerlessness over alcohol versus visiting friends in a bar, Doug defensively replied that he had ordered only club soda. Still, the therapist pointed out, the fact that Doug would place himself in such a situation in the first place was not consistent with his statement that he was powerless over alcohol. She used this analogy:

Say that a man told you he was a gambling addict and that he had lost his house and ran into debt as a result of it. Say he admitted that he was powerless over his urge to gamble and that once he started, he could not be sure he would stop. Suppose he then told you that although he didn't want to gamble any more, he still liked to meet his old gambling buddies for dinner and that the place where they met for dinner was a casino. Now, would you say that this man's actions were consistent with a belief that gambling was a dangerous addictive tendency within him, one that had the power to overpower his own determination not to gamble?

Doug had to admit that in this hypothetical example, the man's actions were not completely consistent with his words: "I guess if he was really afraid of losing everything at a craps table, he wouldn't set foot in a casino." The therapist pointed out that Doug had lost a lot as a result of alcoholism and that if he truly accepted his powerlessness over it, the last place he'd want to hang out would be in a bar. His behavior, the therapist said, was more consistent with resistance to accepting the first step; in other words, more consistent with denial than acceptance. It reflected, in behavioral terms, a belief on Doug's part in the capacity of his individual willpower to overcome the risks inherent in placing himself in situations in which the risk of a slip was high. Doug could see how this was true. "I suppose it's just a hard pill to swallow," he said. "I mean, this idea that my willpower isn't enough. On some level, I've never wanted to accept it."

Spouses and other concerned significant others should be encouraged to observe substance abusers' actions and to compare their actions to what they say. When they discover a discrepancy, this can be a sign of denial. It is *not* necessarily the significant other's responsibility to confront the substance abuser about this each and every time or to break down his or her denial; rather, this awareness of denial is useful in so far as it can validate the client's own thinking in the face of opposition and denial from the addict. It can also help to encourage significant others to continue the process of caring detachment and to not be drawn into the addicts' denial systems.

The objective in this discussion of the various forms of denial is to be sure the client has an understanding of their common theme: *Denial in all of its forms serves to protect the substance abuser from having to acknowledge a progressive loss of control over substance use.* To check that the client understands denial clearly, help him or her to identify several specific examples of denial that his or her loved one has actually used. In each instance, write down what the substance abuser said and what form of denial it represents. This exercise can help to sensitize the codependent to denial when he or she encounters it again.

Example #1. What was said: _____. What form of denial? _____

Example #2. What was said:_____. What form of denial? _____

Example #3. What was said:_____. What form of denial? _____

Help the client to identify any specific examples of discrepancies between the substance abuser's statements about his or her substance use versus his or her actions. This is not usually difficult to do, especially for substance abusers who are still active or those who are in the early stages of recovery.

Example #1. Words:_____ versus actions:_____

Example #2. Words:_____ versus actions:_____

Example #3. Words:_____ versus actions:_____

Denial in Codependents

The process of denial, as it operates in alcoholics and drug addicts, has its parallels in their significant others. The therapist should note this and explain that there can be many reasons why significant others may be as reluctant to face the reality of addiction as are addicts themselves.

To move toward caring detachment, codependents need to become cognizant of two tendencies in particular within themselves. The first is the tendency to buy into the addicts' own denial. This can be explored through open-ended questions such as the following:

> How many times have you bought into your loved one's denial, in other words, believed his or her explanation instead of trusting your own perceptions? Can you give me an example of a time when you believed an excuse you were getting?
>
> What forms of denial are you particularly likely to buy into? For instance, do you tend to accept rationalizations for drinking or using? Are you gullible with respect to a minimizing and maximizing strategy?

When significant others accept addicts' denial, they help to create a kind of conspiracy. Sometimes, they do so simply because they, too, do not want to face the fact that their relationships with their loved ones have in a sense been displaced by other relationships—a commitment between the addicts and alcohol or drugs. By slipping into a conspiracy of denial they, like the addicts, can cling to the comforting illusion that the situations are really not that bad. Conversely, as denial breaks down, the addict and the codependent alike can be flooded with anxiety.

In addition to not wanting to admit that neither they nor the addicts can control substance abuse at that time, guilt and shame are common reasons why significant others may hesitate to face up to the true severity of loved ones' substance abuse problems: guilt that they may somehow be responsible for the problems and shame over the stigma associated with alcoholism and drug addiction. For some, their loved ones' addictions stir up added feelings of shame associated with a parent's addiction. These people may not want to admit to themselves that once again, someone they love has been lost to them through addiction.

Another motive for denial in significant others has to do with a reluctance to accept their own personal limitations. Simply put, *as an addict progressively loses control over substance use, so does his or her significant others.* Many co-dependents doggedly refuse to face this limitation of their own willpower—that they can't stop the addicts from drinking or using—just as addicts refuse to face their limitations even in the throes of addiction. For these people, letting go of the illusion that they can prevent or contain addiction directly parallels the addicts' need to let go of the illusion that they can drink or use like other people. It may be hubris, or it may be anxiety, or perhaps some combination of both that drives this illusion, but in any case, the reality of the codependent's loss of control over the addict directly parallels the reality of the addict's loss of control over substance use. Letting go of any illusion to the contrary is equally important to both parties in the relationship if they are to recover.

Explore the client's motivations for denial by asking questions such as the following:

Have you often wanted to believe that the extent of your loved one's substance abuse was not really so bad?

Did it ever disturb you to think that you might be losing your loved one to alcohol or drugs, in other words, that the relationship with alcohol or drugs was becoming more important than his or her relationship with you?

Have you believed at times that it was in your power somehow to get your loved one to stop or control his or her substance use?

What factors within you might motivate you to want to avoid facing up to the reality of your loved one's addiction and the fact that you are both out of control of his or her substance use? For example:

Would you feel embarrassed or ashamed about it?

Would it mean facing up to a problem of major proportions in your life, one that might prove overwhelming?

Would it remind you of something unpleasant from your own past?

Have you ever felt guilty (i.e., responsible for) your loved one's substance use? In what way do you imagine you could be responsible for it?

How does it make you feel if you think about the idea that you cannot stop your loved one from drinking or using?

▓ Summing Up

Again, sum up the session by asking the client to tell you the most important thing he or she learned from this discussion. You might want to point out that in Al-Anon and Nar-Anon, the client will find people who have shared his or her experience—who, for instance, have had to come to terms with the limits of their willpower and who have found themselves caught with addicts in the webs of denial. These men and women can offer support and guidance both in living with an addict and with beginning the process of recovery.

Recovery Tasks

The recovery tasks to be suggested are as follows:

Meetings

Continue to suggest to the client that she or he attend Al-Anon or Nar-Anon meetings with the specific suggestion that he or she attend a minimum of two meetings per week. Active facilitation, as described earlier, can be used at any time to assist this process.

Suggest to the client that he or she listen particularly closely to two types of members at meetings: newcomers, meaning persons like themselves, and also old-timers, those who have been active in Al-Anon or Nar-Anon for a relatively long time and who impress them; in other words, people they respect and would want to emulate. The goal is for the therapist to encourage the client to begin to bond to the fellowship through contact with these two groups. Old-timers— seasoned Al-Anon or Nar-Anon members—are good candidates for becoming the newcomer's first sponsor.

Telephone Therapy

Make a specific suggestion that the client get the names and phone numbers of two or three same-sex Al-Anon or Nar-Anon members and that he or she try calling and speaking with two such people each week. Suggest that it is best if he or she get the phone numbers of two relative newcomers and two old-timers who have impressed them favorably. If necessary, explain again to the client that this telephone therapy is a long-standing tradition within Al-Anon and Nar-Anon (as well as AA and NA) and that experienced Al-Anon or Nar-Anon members will welcome their interest.

Treatment Note: The Socially Shy Client

If the client seems excessively shy or uneasy about the idea of getting phone numbers or making calls, explore his or her anxiety by asking if this has been a problem for him or her in the past. Most socially anxious people describe themselves as having been shy for most of their lives. It can be reassuring to let the shy client know that many Al-Anon and Nar-Anon members are also shy at first and can relate to this problem and also, that an important tradition within 12-step fellowships is to reach out and connect to others. The therapist might want to either role-play or talk through one such icebreaker phone call. The agenda for these first calls can be simple:

> Hi, my name is _____. I was at the meeting on _____. I'm a newcomer, and I thought I would just call to make contact. Normally, I'm kind of a shy person, but these days, I know I need to start reaching out.

In most cases, this brief intervention will prove sufficient to initiate at least a brief phone conversation and to start the client on the process of building a network of Al-Anon or Nar-Anon contacts.

Readings

The following readings are suggested as a follow-up for this topic:

Al-Anon Faces Alcoholism (Al-Anon, 1985), pages 170-173:"My Brother is an Alcoholic"; pages 147-151:"Al-Anon Helped Me to Understand My Wife's Problem"; pages 246-255:"Other Tools of the Program"

Journal

Encourage the client to continue to make journal entries about his or her reactions to sessions, to meetings, and to readings, and to use these entries as grist for the mill at the next session.

Caring Detachment

As before, the therapist works collaboratively with the client to come up with one or two specific things that she or he can do toward decreasing his or her enabling relationship with the substance abuser and move the relationship instead in the direction of caring detachment. Keep in mind always that detaching as a way of relating to the addict is something that is best shaped incrementally. No matter how minor, a response to the addict that represents caring detachment instead of enabling is likely to elicit a reaction. Caring detachment reflects honesty on the part of the codependent plus a willingness to allow the addict to have the dignity of his or her disease without taking over responsibility for the addiction or for recovery. *Successful detaching almost always disrupts the dynamic status quo in the addict-codependent relationship.*

CHAPTER 11

Topic 5

Enabling

THE GOAL OF THIS SESSION is to explain to the client how denial, as discussed previously (see Topic 4), is connected to enabling as a relational pattern. Both denial and enabling are based in the conscious or unconscious belief that the significant other can somehow control or at least contain a substance abuse problem and its consequences. *Enabling reflects resistance to Step 1 of Al-Anon and Nar-Anon, which concerns acceptance.*

▨ Review

Begin the session as usual by devoting the first 10 minutes to a discussion of the client's experiences since the last session. Ask if she or he has made any journal entries that she or he would like to discuss. Be sure to briefly cover each of the following areas:

Meetings

How many Al-Anon or Nar-Anon meetings did the client attend?

What thoughts and emotional reactions did the client have to meetings? Are there any questions that the therapist can help to answer?

Does the client have any reservations about continuing to attend Al-Anon or Nar-Anon meetings?

Telephone Therapy

> Did the client follow up on the therapist's suggestion to get and use Al-Anon or Nar-Anon members' phone numbers? Is there anything that can be done to facilitate this?

Readings

> Did the client follow up on the suggested readings? What reactions or questions does she or he have?

Caring Detachment

> What action(s) has the client taken since the last session to start or continue the process of moving from enabling toward caring detachment?
>
> What was his or her level of comfort in taking these steps?
>
> What reaction was there from the substance abuser, if any?

▨ New Material

The therapist should be thoroughly familiar with the material that follows and should use it as a guide in engaging the client in a discussion of the concept of enabling.

Enabling can be defined as any and all behaviors by significant others that have unintentionally facilitated the addicts' continued substance use. Enabling, as a relational dynamic between the codependent and the addict, unintentionally promotes the progression of the addict's relationship with alcohol or drugs. At best, enabling maintains the status quo within the addict-codependent relationship, though, over time, it inevitably leads to a diluting of the quality of that relationship.

Often, a hallmark of enabling is that, in one way or another, it helps the drinker or user to avoid or minimize negative consequences related to substance use, be they physical, legal, occupational, or relational consequences. In other words, as the word implies, enablers provide the means, the excuses, and the safety nets that allow the alcoholics or addicts to continue substance use. This is poignantly described in the following description of a mother's response to her teenage daughter's substance use:

> The convulsions she had at home were so thoroughly covered up by me that she could not remember them the next day. I massaged her, poured honey down her throat, soothed her, and applied cold compresses. It proved futile

to tell her what had occurred because, within a short time, the substance use began again. It is now clear to me that it is necessary for the alcoholic to feel the pain. But it was I who bore my daughter's pain. I deprived her of some of the incentive to take constructive action for the consequences of her substance use. In essence, I took on the responsibility and the consequences of her disease. (Al-Anon, 1985, p. 182)

Yet another way to look at enabling is that it represents indulgence or pampering of the addict. It can be motivated out of caring and concern, as in the previous example; alternatively, it may reflect the enabler's own personality and his or her desire to deny the reality of addiction, as the following account by the wife of an alcoholic suggests:

> False pride helped me create a prison in which I lived for the next 20 years. I wanted to be proud of our marriage and our family (we had six sons), so I buried the resentment and began pretending. By the time our sons were in their twenties, one had gone through treatment for chemical dependency. I also realized that three of our other sons were chemical abusers. I didn't want to believe this was happening or that alcohol was the problem. So I kept on pretending, and I played the role of caretaker for the whole family. I assumed it was my job to control them, make them happy, keep them from hurting and out of trouble. The family seemed to agree. Their dependent personalities accepted such mothering and only occasionally did they rebel. (Carolyn W., 1984)

As another example of enabling, consider Elaine, age 55, who held a responsible position and supported two adult sons, both of whom were alcoholics. She had divorced their alcoholic father when the boys were young, not so much because he drank but because he'd been chronically unfaithful. She sought help for a common and understandable reason: chronic frustration in coping with her sons. She was feeling "soul tired," as she put it: discouraged and disheartened. One of her sons was now living with her, was unemployed and unmotivated. The other lived on his own but was also very dependent on her for anything from money for booze to a decent meal.

Elaine asked her therapist outright for a solution to her dilemma and distress. She had no qualms about sharing her feelings of hopelessness and admitting her sense of defeat. She hoped that the therapist would miraculously have an answer. She said that she had been thinking about relocating to another state, just to escape the situation.

The therapist pointed out that because her sons were clearly dependent on her, they would no doubt follow Elaine, even if she did move. She laughed at that, but the point as well taken. The bottom line—the reality of her utter frustration—was clearly well-understood by her and her therapist.

Elaine was a strong enabler. Virtually everything she did supported the status quo and undermined any motivation for either of her sons to change, while allowing their relationships with alcohol and drugs to progress from that of friendship to one of commitment. Her younger son—the one who lived at home—she thought might be on the verge of becoming a slave to cocaine.

Elaine fed and housed her sons, did their laundry, lent them money. It was during her fourth session therapy that Elaine's intense guilt became apparent to her therapist, along with the role that guilt played in her enabling. She was talking about having been a single parent:

> After my divorce, I never did find a man I could believe in enough to want to marry again. It's a common story, I know, but I just seemed to attract more of the same! Anyway, it bothered me at times that the boys never had a proper father. I tried my best never to deny them. I'm the kind of person who hates to say no. I remember one time, though, when my youngest was 10 and he wanted to go to this weekend thing with these older boys, and I said no. I felt he was just too young. He got really upset. It hurt me to say no, but I had to do it. Sometimes, I wonder if that didn't affect him in some way.

How ironic that this mother actually blamed herself for her son's addiction because of one time when she denied him! Of course, to pursue the goal of caring detachment would require her to move in just the opposite direction: to learn to deny more often. Only by doing so could she begin to break the cycle of indulgence and restructure her relationships with her grown sons so as to be that of adult to adult, instead of the parent-child relationships that they'd always been. To accomplish this, it was evident that she would need a great deal of support, not only from the therapist but from the fellowship of Al-Anon.

However it is defined, the bottom line is that enabling serves to mitigate the consequences of alcoholism or drug addiction and thereby it has the (perhaps unintended) effect of allowing the disease to progress. *Without their systems of enablers, most addicts would bottom out more quickly than they otherwise would.*

The therapist should ask the client if she or he has heard the term, "enabling," and if so, what it means to him or her. Check that the client has a clear understanding of this concept in light of the material presented earlier. Reading the preceding passages can be useful as is paraphrasing the definition of enabling given earlier. Last, illustrate enabling by using a few examples such as the following:

Enabling is . . .

- making excuses (covering up) for the substance abuser when she or he is drunk or high and would otherwise get into trouble

- giving an alcoholic "only a little" alcohol, in the hope that she or he won't want any more (or giving a drug abuser "only a little" money when she or he asks for it)

- giving in to demands to "borrow" money, or paying bills that the substance abuser has run up due to impaired judgment or impulsivity when using

- calling in "sick" for the person who in truth is hung over or crashing after drug use

- conspiring with the addict to accept his or her denial in whatever form it takes

- excusing or justifying hostility, abuse, or other inappropriate behavior that results from substance abuse

- accepting guilt-ridden apologies after the fact for harm or damage done while under the influence of alcohol or drugs and believing that it will never happen again

- making runs to liquor stores (or drug dealers) to keep an alcoholic or addict off the street (to avoid arrest or an accident)

- defending an alcoholic or addict to others or apologizing for the addict for inappropriate or irresponsible behavior

- giving an addict liquor or drugs to quiet him or her down or keep the peace

The common theme in all of these examples is that enabling in any of its forms has the effect of helping the alcoholic or drug addict avoid the real issue, which is his or her substance abuse, in large part, by helping to minimize the consequences that would otherwise result from it. In time, the addict-codependent relationship settles into a stable but highly dysfunctional pattern, becoming progressively more of a parent-child than an adult-to-adult relationship. Meanwhile, the substance abuser's relationship with alcohol or drugs deepens.

An irony of enabling is that the consequences that are minimized are the very ones that might help to motivate the substance abuser to think about changing, whereas enabling undermines any such motivation. All the while, the codependent becomes progressively more responsible for the addict, instead of the addict taking responsibility for himself or herself.

Constructing an Enabling Inventory

To be certain that the client clearly understands the concept of enabling and can relate to it in the context of his or her relationship with the substance abuser, elicit several examples of enabling and use them to construct an Enabling

Inventory. A blackboard or flip chart is helpful for this. If neither are available, a large sheet of paper will suffice. Be sure to give the client a copy of the inventory to keep after it is finished.

The Enabling Inventory is a list of specific ways in which the codependent has allowed the substance abuser to do the following:

Gain access to alcohol or drugs

    Example #1 _____

    Example #2 _____

Minimize or avoid physical, occupational, or relational consequences of substance use

    Example #1 _____

    Example #2 _____

Progress in his or her relationship with alcohol or drugs

    Example #1 _____

    Example #2 _____

Enabling and Denial

Enabling of substance abusers by significant others can be thought of as a complementary process to denial in addicts, in that the one supports the other. The underlying dynamic in denial and enabling is that both individuals resist facing the reality of progressive loss of control over substance use. The potential alcoholic, for example, continues to hold on to the illusion that he or she can drink like "normal" people, despite increasing evidence to the contrary. Meanwhile, the codependent either continues to believe his or her same myth—that the addict can drink or use like the nonaddict—or else to believe that he or she can get the addict to stop drinking or contain the damage caused by addiction.

This latter thought—be it conscious or merely implied in the significant other's actions—rests on the assumption that a concerned significant other can indeed somehow control an addict's substance abuse. In reality, as addiction progresses, significant others who are caught up in an enabling dynamic take more and more responsibility for the substance abusers in their lives, who in turn become increasingly irresponsible and immature. The addict-codependent relationship thereby moves progressively toward that of parent to child as the addict's relationship to alcohol or drugs becomes more and more intimate and committed.

It is important, from the point of view of motivating significant others to give Al-Anon or Nar-Anon or both a try, that they understand, on both an intellectual and a gut level, this central concept of enabling, how it parallels denial, and how it undermines any possibility for recovery. *If the client appears to be having difficulty grasping this concept, the facilitator may need to return to it again and again in future sessions, each time, illustrating it concretely through the client's self-reported actions and contrasting it with what detaching would look like.*

The Dynamics of Enabling

Enabling is fairly obvious as it is revealed in behavior. In contrast, the underlying motivations for enabling may be complex and less apparent. Although it typically has the effect of allowing the addict to drink or use, most people enable not because they actually want the addicts to continue substance use but out of desires to protect or shelter the addicts, desires to preserve relationships, feelings of guilt, or senses of duty. The motives for enabling are benign and loving, even though they have the effect in the long run of being mutually destructive to the addict, the codependent, and their relationship.

It can be useful in promoting caring detachment to get the client to think about and identify some of his or her underlying motivations for enabling. Often, one or more of the following statements will turn out to apply to most clients' experiences:

> On some level, I keep thinking that it will make a difference if I keep on doing what I've been doing.
>
> I feel that this is the only way to save our relationship.
>
> I think I will eventually convince him (her) to stop.
>
> I'm afraid of what will happen to him (her) if I stop doing what I'm doing.
>
> I feel partly responsible for the problem.

How do enablers feel? Often, they feel guilty because they secretly worry that they have somehow caused or contributed to the problems. This is a hidden fear that many alcoholics and addicts play on to promote enabling. Many partners and family members of addicts report deep feelings of self-doubt about their adequacy in their relationship with the substance abuser.

Enablers are often fearful and anxious because they don't know what could happen if they let go. What would be the impact, for example, on a marriage, or on a family's financial security, if they stopped enabling?

Enablers also experience considerable frustration and feel angry because the addict won't change, won't listen to advice, and continues to drink or use. Like the addicts, they find themselves repeating scenes that they'd hoped would never happen again: calling in sick for the hungover husband, making excuses to family or friends for inappropriate behavior, cleaning up messes, and so on.

Sooner or later, enablers experience hopelessness and feel depressed as a result of continued substance use and the progressive unmanageability of not only the addicts' lives but also their own and their relationships. As an inner sense of hopelessness sets in, many spouses eventually write off both the addicts and the relationships, emotionally speaking, even if they don't actually divorce. They give up seeking intimacy, love, and even reliability from their spouse, accepting instead his or her primary commitment to alcohol or drugs.

In the end, feelings of alienation take root as estrangement hardens. Eventually, this state of affairs can undermine the spiritual, psychological, and physical health of the significant other. Not a few have turned to alcohol or drugs themselves as a compensation for the quiet desperation and loneliness that plagues them.

Try to get the client to identify the various emotions he or she feels with respect to the substance abuse problem. Does he or she feel any of the following?

Guilty, because of fear that he or she is somehow responsible

Anxious, because life is becoming progressively more unmanageable as a result of substance abuse

Angry, because his or her efforts at stopping or containing the problem have been frustrated

Depressed, because things seem out of control

Hopeless and ready to give up on love, intimacy, and commitment

Alienated, because his or her profound sense of defeat has hardened into resignation at having lost a relationship to alcohol or drugs

These are all feelings and states that clients will eventually discover others at Al-Anon and Nar-Anon meetings have also experienced. However, newcomers are especially prone to sinking into hopeless despair and therefore are vulnerable to dropping out of Al-Anon or Nar-Anon prematurely if they keep such feelings to themselves, as opposed to sharing them at meetings and opening themselves up to support. Being able to acknowledge and express such feelings to the therapist, therefore, particularly early on in his or her involvement in a 12-step fellowship, can be critical to a client's ability to bond to the fellowship in the long run.

▓ Summing Up

Ask the client to summarize what she or he got out of this session. Particular attention should be paid (a) to see that clients understand enabling and can identify at least a few specific ways they have enabled their addicts, (b) to clients' abilities to identify their possible motives for enabling, and (c) to helping clients express their feelings about their own relationships with the substance abusers as well as the substance abusers' relationships with drugs or alcohol.

▓ Recovery Tasks

The suggested recovery tasks for this topic are as follows:

Meetings

Continue to suggest that the client attend Al-Anon and Nar-Anon meetings, with the specific suggestion that he or she attend two meetings per week. Active facilitation, as described earlier, can be used at any time to assist this process.

Again, suggest to the client that he or she listen particularly closely to two types of members at meetings: newcomers, like themselves, and old-timers who have been active in Al-Anon or Nar-Anon for a relatively long time and who impress him or her as people they would like to know better. The goal for the therapist is to consistently encourage and coach the client to establish a connection to other newcomers as well as these seasoned Al-Anon or Nar-Anon members so as to facilitate the process of bonding to the fellowship.

Telephone Therapy

Continue to encourage the client to get and give phone numbers and establish a network of Al-Anon or Nar-Anon contacts. Use role-playing if necessary to facilitate this.

Readings

The following readings are recommended, along with any others that the client may have discovered—for example, by going to meetings.

Al-Anon Faces Alcoholism (Al-Anon, 1985), pages 31-36:"Detachment and Growth"; pages 134-139:"I Learned to Love"

Caring Detachment

Suggest one or two specific things the client can do to decrease his or her enabling of the substance abuser and increase caring detachment. Continue to reinforce these efforts to change as ones that will, in time, change the nature of the addict-codependent relationship, moving it from an unhealthy dependency (parent-child) toward mutual respect (adult-adult). Help the client to identify and work through any feelings of guilt or anxiety that might undermine his or her efforts to detach.

CHAPTER 12

Topic 6
Acceptance

THE GOAL OF THIS SESSION is to explore the first step of Al-Anon and Nar-Anon, which concerns acceptance. In the discussion of new material, the therapist will ask the client how she or he has tried to control or contain the addiction process, how that has worked, and whether the client is now ready to try another way. Reactions to powerlessness and unmanageability will be explored in depth here to enhance the client's motivation to use Al-Anon or Nar-Anon.

▨ Review

Begin the session, as in previous ones, by devoting about 10 minutes to checking in with the client. Aside from inquiring about relevant journal entries that the client might want to share, be sure to touch on each of the following areas:

Meetings

How many Al-Anon or Nar-Anon meetings did the client attend since the last session?

What thoughts and emotional reactions has the client had to meetings? Has he or she found people to identify with?

Are there issues that could be addressed that would facilitate the client's active participation in and bonding with Al-Anon or Nar-Anon?

Does the client have any reservations about continuing to attend Al-Anon or Nar-Anon meetings? Can any of these be worked through?

Treatment Note: Focusing on Similarities

Often, individuals who consistently report feeling unconnected or uncomfortable at meetings are doing one of two things that undermine the bonding process. First, they may be attending a meeting that does not happen to be conducive to identification. One couple, for example, the parents of a young adult drug addict, found themselves unable to relate to the one Nar-Anon meeting that was available in their area. Virtually all of the other members of this group were either the wives or girlfriends of heroin addicts, and most were considerably younger than they were. On learning this, their counselor suggested they try a couple of Al-Anon meetings, including one that the counselor knew was specifically for parents. It was a little more inconvenient, but the results were very positive. As they put it, this couple had now found a home base. Indeed, every concerned significant other, like every addict, needs to be able to find a home group to use as a foundation for his or her recovery. Twelve-step fellowships are highly diverse. There are so many different groups and different formats that it is all but impossible in most areas to *not* be able to find at least one that a newcomer could feel some identity with.

Difficulties with bonding can also stem from a significant other's tendency to focus attention on group members who he or she do not relate to, while largely ignoring those they could identify with. This may reflect a conscious or unconscious resistance to bonding, in which case, the significant other can be expected to persist in focusing on members he or she sees as very different from himself or herself, despite the counselor's best efforts to work this through. Alternatively, this problem has also been found to be correctable in many cases through effective coaching by a skilled counselor. One common problem for some newcomers is a kind of compulsion to focus all of their attention on another group member who irritates or annoys them in some way. On further inquiry, the counselor may discover that they do this in other group situations as well. One newcomer to Al-Anon, for example, expressed frustration with a male member of the group she was going to whom she thought was very sexist. Each time she went, she found herself sitting in the meeting perseverating over everything this man said. Meanwhile, when asked by her counselor, she could never recall much of what anyone else had said. The counselor suggested that the newcomer either try some different meetings or else focus on what others were saying and then report back in their next session. The newcomer took the second option, with good results. At the next session, she was even able to laugh at herself. She told the counselor,

> You know, I realized that there were a lot of other good people at that meeting, but I wasn't open to them. Instead, I kept fixating on this guy. Then, I realized that I was having trouble letting go of him, just like I have trouble letting go of my husband!

Another newcomer, a man, kept complaining to his therapist that there were so many women at the meetings he went to and that none of the men there was a professional like himself. He was advised to try looking beyond these differences and to try focussing instead on identifying with the core story of codependence, which has to do with progressive loss of control, unmanageability, and eventual alienation from the addict. Conversely, recovery in codependents is a story of slow but steady movement toward caring detachment. In this case, that meant, in part, allowing his wife to have the dignity of her disease: to experience its natural consequences, which included his changed feelings for her (which for years he largely avoided thinking about and had never shared with her) and to work on moving from the dependency of an enabling relationship toward the mutual respect that comes from caring detachment.

As he began to focus on the members' shared core story, instead of what sex they were or what they did for a living, this newcomer found that he could very easily identify and bond with this group and use it as a base of support for detaching.

Telephone Therapy

Has the client gotten and used any phone numbers? If not, what is the source of the resistance? Can anything be done to facilitate this?

Readings

Did the client follow up on any suggested readings? What reactions or questions does she or he have?

Has the client discovered any new readings that she or he would like to share?

New Material

Begin the discussion by reading the first step of Al-Anon aloud: "*We admitted we were powerless over alcohol—that our lives had become unmanageable*" (Al-Anon, 1985, p. 236).

Point out that this step, which is identical to the first step of AA (as well as that of NA, which simply substitutes the word *drugs* for *alcohol*), includes two related concepts that are central to why 12-step fellowships like Al-Anon, Nar-Anon, AA, and NA exist. These concepts are powerlessness and unmanageability, which in turn are related in that it is increasing powerlessness over substance use that makes life progressively more unmanageable for addicts and their significant others alike.

Discuss the foregoing ideas with the client, beginning with a discussion of powerlessness.

Powerlessness

Psychologically and emotionally, the concept of powerlessness is a charged one. Powerlessness is threatening. As was pointed out earlier, it is an idea that runs counter in particular to our cultural ethic, which embraces radical individualism and stresses individual achievement over interdependence and collective effort. In this cultural context, admitting powerlessness over anything, including substance use, can be seen as a crushing personal defeat (and something to be ashamed of). It is, in fact, regarded that way by many addicts and codependents. On the other hand, accepting and admitting powerlessness can be seen simply as a statement of humility: that personal willpower alone has not been successful in one's efforts to effectively limit or control substance use and that negative consequences of substance use continue to accrue.

Engage the client in a discussion of powerlessness and these two very different ways of approaching it. The goal of this dialogue is to help the client identify which reaction—horror and shame or humble acceptance—he or she has to the idea of admitting powerlessness. A useful context for this discussion is the many ways in which the client has tried to control or contain his or her partner's substance use. Open-ended questions, such as the following, can be useful for this purpose:

Can you remember how you reacted when the thought first occurred to you that _____ had or was developing a substance use problem? What did you think? What was your emotional reaction?

How have you tried to control or limit _____'s substance use? Describe several specific things you've done. (Note: The therapist might want to prompt the client here by mentioning common things that significant others typically do, such as threatening, removing alcohol or drugs from the house, arguing, pleading, warning, etc.).

What was the outcome of each of the efforts you made to get _____ to stop substance use?

How does it make you feel when your efforts don't work?

Have you started to feel powerless over _____'s substance use?

Some people have a much harder time than others admitting that they are powerless over things, including being powerless to control someone else's substance abuse. How difficult is this for you to admit?

Treatment Note: Powerlessness Versus Helplessness

It can be very important to include in this discussion of powerlessness some discussion of the difference between powerlessness versus helplessness. This point has been made before, but it is worth repeating again now: The client needs to appreciate the fact that although she or he may be powerless to force the drinker or user to stop, she or he is not helpless when it comes to stopping the enabling and changing the dynamics within the relationship that only serve to prolong the problem. Significant others are also not helpless with respect to learning to take care of their own health and well-being. That is an integral part of caring detachment as opposed to enabling. Active involvement in Al-Anon or Nar-Anon or both is the preferred source of support to work toward both of these goals.

Unmanageability

Life for both addicts and their loved ones becomes progressively unmanageable as addiction progresses through its several stages from social use to compulsive use of alcohol or drugs or both. Unmanageability is the direct result of growing powerlessness over substance use.

The therapist can use the following case example (or another one drawn from his or her experience that serves to illustrate the same points) to facilitate a discussion of unmanageability.

Bob and Kathy, a couple married for 20 years, went to a counselor, ostensibly for help with marital difficulties. Though it was initially obscured by discussions and arguments about money, children, and sex, it became apparent after a while that Bob had a significant drinking problem that needed to be evaluated. He was asked to come in individually for a session to talk about this. Reluctantly, he agreed.

It turned out that Bob had several signs of alcohol dependency. He had a powerful tolerance, drank daily, and had experienced a number of drinking-related consequences, not the least of which was a seriously strained marriage. He had hypertension serious enough to require medication. Last, the counselor discovered that he was in trouble at work as a consequence of drinking—a consequence he'd kept secret from his wife. All things considered, Bob had a commitment to alcohol that was clearly taking priority more and more over his commitments at home and at work.

Bob was reluctant to change the focus of therapy from his troubled marriage to his drinking. This was interpreted as part of his denial. He was assured that his concerns about the marriage were legitimate and would be dealt with; but first, the counselor said, he needed to do something about his drinking or risk losing his job, possibly his marriage, and definitely his health.

The story of Bob's private struggle for control over alcohol was a testament to stubborn determination as much as it was a classic story of the power of addiction.

Having started out sipping beers stolen from the refrigerator as a youth barely 10 years old, Bob had been drinking continuously for 30 years. But things didn't get bad, he said, until after he was married and the kids were born. Two things happened then. First, he felt obligated to stay in a job that paid well but that he had previously intended to leave. Second, his relationship with Kathy, in his words, became diluted as a consequence of the demands of family life.

It was around this time, after his younger child, a daughter, was born, that Bob developed the habit of having a cocktail or two every night after work and before dinner. For a long time, Kathy went along with this, though she did notice that a cocktail or two eventually became three, four, or more. Her own father had been a drinker and so for a long time, Bob's behavior did not strike Kathy as particularly abnormal. Ironically, she took his ability to drink others under the table—in other words, his tolerance—to be a good thing. In her naivete, she believed that his ability to hold his liquor was actually a sign that Bob could not become addicted.

As time went on, the process of addiction gradually set in. Instead of eating in the company cafeteria, Bob found himself liking to go out for lunch two or three times a week. Of course, he'd have a couple of beers every time. By the time he got home, he was anxious to "relax"—his euphemism for having cocktails. Kathy and the kids soon found that anything that stood between Bob and his cocktails made him irritable. He didn't want to be bothered with problems until he was "relaxed." Of course, by the time he was relaxed, Bob was also intoxicated. That made him emotionally unstable and prone to losing his temper. So the rest of the family eventually learned to avoid him. Kathy took to solving most of the household problems by herself or else let them go. The kids, meanwhile, led their own lives and had minimal communication with their father.

Though he was hesitant to admit it for a long time, privately Bob had struggled long and hard (and ultimately unsuccessfully) to control his drinking. He hadn't wanted to be like his own father: a quiet drunk who was less flamboyant than Bob in his drinking but who had liked his liquor nonetheless and who had also been a social isolate and a nonfactor, as Bob described his role as a parent.

Even though Bob had never read the Big Book, the methods he eventually disclosed that he had tried in his long struggle to control his drinking sounded like something right out of it: drinking only wine, drinking only beer (no cocktails) at lunch, drinking from a smaller glass, adding more ice cubes to his cocktails, and so on. All the while, he was conscious on some level of gradually losing control, yet he continued to convince himself that he was really all right.

By the time he and Kathy came for marital therapy, Bob had managed to fall 2 years behind on his tax returns and owed the government several thousand dollars. According to Kathy, the house they lived in was falling apart faster and faster on account of maintenance projects he refused to hire someone to do but kept putting off doing himself. Their son, who had just turned 18, was failing half of his courses in college;

meanwhile, according to Bob, his daughter hated him and alternately fought with and ridiculed him. He had not gotten a merit raise for 3 years at work, and his job evaluations, once outstanding, were now routinely average. His boss was openly critical of his work, and Bob was convinced that the man was out to get him. Worst of all, he had suffered the humiliation of being called on the carpet as a result of having alcohol on his breath and had been warned that a second such incident would lead to disciplinary action. On top of all this, Kathy was sexually turned off, which left Bob feeling not only frustrated but filled with self-pity that only made him want to drink all the more.

◆

Like Bob, every alcoholic's and addict's life is a story of increasing powerlessness and unmanageability. As the first step of Al-Anon and Nar-Anon as well as this story makes clear, this unmanageability affects not only the alcoholic or addict but all those who are close to him or her.

Engage the client in a discussion of how his or her loved one's alcohol or drug abuse has made both of their lives increasingly unmanageable. If necessary, prompt the client's memory with information you've gathered during earlier sessions. By this point in the program, the therapist should have a fairly thorough knowledge of the client's relationship with the substance abuser and should have ample concrete examples of progressive unmanageability. The therapist may want to actually list several ways in which she or he believes the client's life has become increasingly unmanageable.

Treatment Note: Acceptance and Depression

Before going on to discuss recovery tasks, the therapist might want to take some time to check in with the client regarding his or her emotional state at this point. Acceptance of one's powerlessness over addiction carries with it the potential to elicit feelings of depression and, in extreme cases, despair. This makes sense if one considers that although denial tends to promote enabling, it also protects the codependent from the harsh reality of addiction and powerlessness. When the wall of denial falls, significant others may experience relief but also intense anxiety. Check this out. Although it is important to validate se (and not avoid) some anxiety and sadness in the client—which is a realistic reaction to Step 1—it is also important not to allow the client to sink into hopelessness. If necessary, point out again that powerlessness is not synonymous with helplessness.

If there is a sense that the client may be feeling helpless and hopeless, take special care to emphasize that Al-Anon and Nar-Anon were founded to help significant others of substance abusers help one another deal with precisely what the client is going through now. If the client has been attending Al-Anon or Nar-Anon, the therapist would of course encourage him or her to continue. On the other hand, if the client has been resistant to Al-Anon or Nar-Anon, this is a perfect time to urge him or her to give it a try, in the interest of reaching out as opposed to going it alone.

Recovery Tasks

The following are the recommended recovery tasks for this topic:

Meetings

Encourage the client to continue going to meetings.

Treatment Note: Variety

Check to see whether the client is attending different meetings and also meeting as wide a range of Al-Anon or Nar-Anon members as possible, including newcomers and old-timers. Encourage the client to begin to look for one or two people (of the same sex as themselves) who have been involved in Al-Anon or Nar-Anon for at least 2 years and who impress him or her as having learned to face alcoholism successfully. This will be used soon to help the client select a temporary sponsor if she or he does not get one spontaneously.

Telephone Therapy

Continue to encourage the client to take advantage of the telephone to develop a network of Al-Anon or Nar-Anon friends. These friends will come in handy if and when a crisis occurs. Remind the client, When you need a friend, you don't want to be calling a stranger.

Journal

Remind the client to keep making use of the journal to record thoughts and reactions for later discussion if she or he has been doing so. It is not too late for the client to start journaling now, if she or he hasn't done so before.

Readings

Suggested readings to follow up on this topic are as follows:

Al-Anon Faces Alcoholism (Al-Anon, 1985), pages 113-119: "I Belong to Something"; pages 180-186: "A Mother of a Teenaged Alcoholic"

Encourage the client to read other Al-Anon stories of his or her choice and to share them with you.

Caring Detachment

Working collaboratively with the client, come up with one or two specific ideas for things that she or he can do to begin to decrease enabling the substance abuser and increase caring detachment.

CHAPTER 13

Topic 7

Caring Detachment

T HE SUBJECT OF THIS SESSION is caring detachment. Analogous to sobriety in substance abusers, caring detachment can be thought of as a primary goal for significant others. Although working on detaching has been a focus throughout this treatment program, in this session, the therapist pays special attention to identifying any issues that stand in the way of the significant other relating to the substance abuser in this way.

Review

Begin the session, as before, by devoting the first 10 minutes to a discussion of the client's experiences since the last session. Ask whether she or he has made any journal entries to discuss. Then, as usual, briefly touch on each of the following areas:

Meetings

How many Al-Anon or Nar-Anon meetings did the client attend? At this point, has he or she begun to bond with the fellowship? If not, what might be standing in the way of the bonding process?

Does the client have any reservations at this point about continuing to attend Al-Anon or Nar-Anon meetings? Can these be worked through in any way?

Telephone Therapy

> Has the client gotten and used any phone numbers? Is there anything that can be done to facilitate this?

Readings

> Did the client follow up on the suggested readings?
>
> What reactions or questions does she or he have?

Detaching

> What progress has the client made since the last session to start or continue the process of relating to the substance abuser through caring detachment? How has his or her behavior changed in relation to the substance abuser? What has his or her level of comfort been in making these changes?
>
> What reaction, if any, has there been to these changes on the part of the client from the substance abuser?

New Material

Detaching can be thought of as the opposite of enabling. It is very different, however, from either alienation or rejection of the substance abuser. Caring detachment is, in fact, very loving. It can also be thought of as the opposite of unhealthy dependency, in that a *relationship based on mutual caring detachment could be characterized as interdependent, as opposed to the dependency that addiction creates*. It is a relationship between equals (i.e., adult to adult), in contrast to the typical addict-codependent dynamic, which parallels that of child to adult. It is based on mutual support and respect, allowing each partner the dignity of their choices.

As addiction progresses, significant others—especially spouses—become increasingly burdened with feelings of responsibility for their substance abusers. Slowly but surely, many move into a parental role; meanwhile, the addict regresses toward a more and more infantile state. The goal in recovery for the codependent is to make gradual changes in the way she or he relates to the addict so as to move the relationship back to the level of adult-to-adult. Doing so leads to improved self-esteem and mental health for codependents. It can relieve them of much of the burden of shame and guilt that often is the ultimate result of their unsuccessful efforts to control the substance abusers. It can also provide relief from the feelings of rejection and the low self-esteem associated with losing a loved one to addiction. Last, and although that is not its primary intent, caring detachment frequently motivates the addict in the long run to consider changing.

The following quote from *Al-Anon Faces Alcoholism* (Al-Anon, 1985) can be used as the starting point for a discussion of caring detachment.

> "Detach!" we are told in Al-Anon. This does not mean detaching ourselves, and our love and compassion, from the alcoholic. Detachment, in the Al-Anon sense, means to realize we are individuals. We are not bound morally to shoulder the alcoholic's responsibilities. (p. 54)

Ask the client to describe to you what his or her idea of enabling is and then, to contrast enabling with caring detachment. Make sure that each of the following points are covered at some point in this discussion:

Enabling and caring detachment refer to different ways of relating to the substance abuser.

Caring detachment can be thought of as the opposite of enabling. Whereas enabling protects or cushions the alcoholic or addict from the natural consequences of substance abuse and preserves the status quo in the addict-codependent relationship, detachment—at least, in part—means allowing the alcoholic or addict to face those consequences, and it tends to upset the relational status quo.

Detachment is based on the idea of each party in a relationship taking responsibility for himself or herself, while still feeling love and concern for the other. Another way to think of it is as allowing the substance abuser to have the dignity of his or her disease without someone else taking it on.

The typical codependent-addict relationship is one of parent to child, with the addict's dependency extending beyond an unhealthy dependence on alcohol or drugs to include an unhealthy dependence on the significant other.

In the long run, the significant other's inability to contain the addiction process, combined with the experience of losing a loved one to alcohol or drugs, leads to resentment, shame, and guilt in the significant other and ultimately, to alienation in the relationship. By moving the addict-codependent relationship from one based on enabling to one based on caring detachment, the significant other can be released from these feelings.

Just as it is important to clarify what detachment is, it is important to clarify what it is not. Many loved ones of substance abusers, when they hear the word "detachment" or hear others in Al-Anon talking about "letting go" or "turning over" the addict, wrongly conclude that they are being urged to reject or even divorce the substance abuser. This is, in fact, not at all the case. Caring detachment is based in love, not rejection. One can love someone deeply yet allow them to take responsibility for themselves. That, basically, is what caring detachment is. To achieve it, however, especially after a long-standing pattern of dependency has been established in a relationship, is not easy. To move toward caring detachment, the client needs to be helped to overcome any barriers that stand in the way.

Barriers to Detaching

Detaching makes sense to most people; yet on a practical level, many of these same people find it hard to integrate a detached attitude into their behavior. They shy away from allowing the alcoholic or drug addict to experience and deal with whatever consequences substance use brings his or her way. They continue to relate to the addict as though she or he was a dependent child. Why is this so?

The most common barriers to effective detachment are guilt, anxiety, and misplaced love, all of which usually have one or more of these sources:

Confusing love for someone else with responsibility for his or her actions

Believing that allowing the alcoholic to experience negative consequences is somehow unloving or cruel

Believing that it is possible, through love or through plain willpower, to control or change another person's obsession

Feeling that somehow you have caused the addiction

Fear that not protecting the addict will lead to even greater disaster

Discuss these possible barriers to detachment with the client. Guilt that stems from feeling disloyal or cruel can be worked through by acknowledging the positive motives for enabling, also pointing out how enabling is defeating for both the substance abuser and the significant other in the long run, and how it actually sets the stage for a substance use problem to get worse instead of better. Check to see whether this is an issue for the client and if so, whether his or her guilt can be relieved by shifting the focus to the long-run risks of enabling as opposed to its short-term benefits.

Next, read and discuss the following Al-Anon statement with the client:

Learning to detach is a great kindness to ourselves and to the chemically dependent person, and well worth overcoming the obstacles in the beginning. One reward of detachment is that it frees us to grow, to "live and let live. (Carolyn W., 1984, p. 5)

Confusing love with responsibility is an easy thing to do, but it is dangerous to the growth of both parties in a relationship. This issue can be approached through a role-reversal technique. Ask the client if she or he believes that the reverse is true: that someone else should take responsibility for what she or he does or for consequences that result from his or her own actions. Ask if that is a good attitude for parents to take toward their children, for friends to take toward each other, or for spouses to have.

Most people are able see the wisdom in caring detachment, though a few will be troubled by some lingering feeling that it is somehow disloyal or unloving. These people's idea of love may be very close to what others would call mutual dependency. Even some of those who do see the virtues in detaching, though, may still need a great deal of coaching and support from the therapist as well as from others in Al-Anon or Nar-Anon in learning to let go of the substance abuser. By bonding to a 12-step fellowship, they can get the caring support, encouragement, and concrete advice that they will need over the long run to change the ingrained dynamics of their relationships with the substance abusers.

Holding on to the (sometimes unconscious) belief that "love can cure all" or that one person's willpower can substitute for another's may be the most tenacious form of resistance to detaching. A frank and respectful dialogue around this issue may help a reluctant client put his or her own beliefs in perspective and set the stage for learning to live and let live, as the preceding statement advocates. It is, after all, not possible for us to substitute our will for someone else's. And even if we could succeed in such a feat, what would that mean for the growth and development of the other person? Most likely, it would stifle any possibility for such growth.

Ask the client to think of two specific situations that might arise and to identify enabling versus detached responses in each one, as in the following example.

An alcoholic wakes up hung over and leaves for work over an hour late, for the third time in as many weeks.

Enabling Response: The client calls in with an excuse for the alcoholic.

Detached Response: The client lets the alcoholic deal with his or her employer, refusing to act as a middleman.

Help the client to come up with two additional examples. If possible, draw on his or her personal experience with the substance abuser:

Situation #1: _____

Enabling Response: _____

Detached Response: _____

*   *   *

Situation #2: _____

Enabling Response: _____

Detached Response: _____

Treatment Note: The Angry Codependent

I once heard the angry father of an alcoholic son make the following comment: "I'm detached from Michael, alright. I don't ever want to see him again!"

Angry and alienated, significant others can sometimes take the concept of detaching to justify their anger and use it as a rationale for outright rejection of the addict. Although the client will no doubt find validation for feelings of anger and alienation at Al-Anon or Nar-Anon meetings, she or he will not in general find support for using those feelings as a justification for rejection. Similarly, a spouse may find support for an eventual decision to separate from an addict but not in anger or vengeance. What people will find through Al-Anon and Nar-Anon is support for caring detachment and for taking care of themselves.

Al-Anon and Nar-Anon, like AA and NA, believe that alcoholics are sick people, not bad people. From this perspective, angry rejection is misplaced. Al-Anon and Nar-Anon strongly advocate a "live and let live" attitude in their publications. Instead of rejection, one finds strong support for turning over the addict to one's Higher Power while taking care of one's own physical, spiritual, and mental health.

The therapist should approach the issue of a client's pent-up frustration and anger directly, for underlying such feelings, there is usually a great deal of pain. It is important to validate such feelings as well as feelings of alienation. They are, after all, understandable. The therapist can also acknowledge that some addict-codependent relationships end eventually in divorce or loss of contact as a consequence of substance abuse. At the same time, the therapist should make the point that the Al-Anon and Nar-Anon approach to relationships emphasizes honesty and detachment but not hatred or vindictiveness. These fellowships recognize the pain and hopelessness that lie beneath the anger and alienation.

The goal for Al-Anon and Nar-Anon members is to stop living the alcoholics' lives and start living their own. The more a significant other is able to do this, the more his or her resentment is likely to subside. Caring detachment, as illustrated earlier, is characterized in part by certain behaviors, but more deeply, it is based in a system of values and an approach to relationships that emphasizes self-respect and dignity. By shifting the focus from the addict to the client, the 12-step approach opens the ways to emotional healing and renewed personal growth.

Summing Up

Remind the client that in future sessions, you will be interested to hear about progress that she or he is making in learning to detach. Specifically, you will be interested in hearing about how he or she has begun to think less about the substance user and more about himself or herself. Similarly, you will be interested in learning what progress he or she has made in not protecting the substance abuser from the natural consequences of his or her alcohol or drug use.

Suggest that substance abusers usually notice and react to changes in the way that others relate to them and that you will be available to talk about this when it happens. However, point out that it will be even more important for the client to discuss it with Al-Anon or Nar-Anon friends. For this reason, having a network of such friends, who the client sees regularly at meetings and also talks to on the phone, becomes more and more important.

Ask the client to summarize what she or he got out of this session and what changes, if any, she or he thinks she or he needs to work toward in the relationship with the substance abuser.

Treatment Note: The Progression of Addiction

One needs to appreciate how denial—in the addict and the significant other alike—can be tenacious. It would not be unusual, for example, for a significant other, even at this stage in the program and in the face of overwhelming evidence to the contrary, to persist in the belief that his or her loved one can somehow control his or her use of alcohol or drugs. As one wife put it, "In my head, I tell myself he's an alcoholic and an addict, but another part of me still wants to know why he just can't give up the drugs and have just a couple of beers now and then." As evidence in support of her belief, she cited the fact that her husband was in fact able to limit himself to a couple of beers about one-third of the times that he drank. However, the rest of the time, he'd get completely drunk. And when he used cocaine, he invariably consumed his entire supply, despite his constant intention to save some for later.

The therapist responded to this woman by pointing out that there was not a sharp line separating one stage of substance use from another and that although her husband seemed clearly to be a habitual user, it was not completely clear that he was as yet a compulsive user. In other words, although he had a clear commitment to alcohol and cocaine (one that interfered with his commitments at home and at work), he was not as yet a slave to them. Rather than attempting to argue with this client over just how much control her husband still had over his use, the therapist emphasized that addiction was progressive: that the negative consequences of her husband's drinking and drug abuse had been accruing for several years, that it was already a major problem, and that the client had not been successful at initiating any significant change, much less a halt, in the process so far.

The wife agreed that what the therapist said made sense. She continued going to both Al-Anon and Nar-Anon meetings. In time, she got a sponsor and continued the process of caring detachment that had begun to elicit some definite reactions from her husband.

If resistance to Step 1 (acceptance of loss of control over alcohol or drug use) is evident at all at this point in treatment, it can be useful for the therapist to check again as to what the client thinks about the substance abuser's stage of use and to compare it to what the client thought when the assessment was first done, especially in light of any new information that has emerged in the course of treatment.

Recovery Tasks

The following are the suggested recovery tasks for this topic:

Meetings

Ask the client to continue to attend two to three Al-Anon or Nar-Anon meetings per week and to journal about his or her reactions. Remind the client about the importance of building a network of Al-Anon or Nar-Anon friends and to nurture that network through phone contacts. The purpose of this, again, is simple: The therapist will not always be there, and it is much better to call a friend than a stranger when a crisis occurs.

Sponsorship

Ask the client to begin talking to other Al-Anon or Nar-Anon members about sponsorship. By now, some clients may have already bonded to the fellowship and have selected a sponsor. If this is so, the therapist merely needs to reinforce this move toward bonding with the fellowship and inquire briefly about how the client selected this person as a sponsor and what this relationship is like: how often they talk, what the sponsor advises, and so forth

If the client has not as yet selected a sponsor, explain that one goal of this program is to help him or her select a temporary sponsor and that you will be discussing this more in the next session. Between now and then, though, the client should give some thought to which Al-Anon or Nar-Anon members he or she most respects, who have had experiences at least somewhat similar to his or her own, and who might be potential sponsors.

Readings

These are the recommended readings to follow up on this topic:

Al-Anon Faces Alcoholism (Al-Anon, 1985), pages 31-36: "Detachment and Growth"; pages 255-257: "Sponsorship"

Al-Anon (n.d.) pamphlet, *So You Love An Alcoholic*

Caroline W. (Hazelden, 1984), *Detaching With Love*

Caring Detachment

In collaboration with the client, the therapist should suggest one or two specific things that she or he can do to decrease his or her enabling of the substance abuser and increase caring detachment.

CHAPTER 14
Topic 8
Surrender

I N THIS SESSION, the therapist focuses in on Steps 2 and 3 of Al-Anon and Nar-Anon and the concept of *surrender*. Key issues for discussion include the notion of working the Al-Anon and Nar-Anon 12-step program and turning over the fate of the addict to a Higher Power, permitting the natural conse-quences of substance abuse to occur without interference, and allowing the substance abuser to make his or her own choices as to what to do about it; in other words, allowing the addict to have the dignity of his disease. In doing this, the significant other must have (or be able to find) the faith that this is the best course of action in the long run. The source of this faith may be spiritual; alternatively, significant others may elect to place their faith in the collective wisdom of Al-Anon and Nar-Anon and in those peers who have made progress in recovering from codependence.

Whatever the source of one's faith, it is clearly necessary if one is to have the courage to surrender. That surrender, in turn, opens the way to change for the significant other and indirectly, for the substance abuser as well, as a result of changes in the addict-codependent relationship. Surrender, when it is achieved, often leads to a profound sense of relief in significant others. The guilt and shame that many loved ones of substance abusers carry is a burden that is lifted from them through surrender. Some have likened surrender to a spiritual awakening.

▨ Review

Begin the session by checking in with the client with respect to their experiences since the last session. Ask about any journal entries that she or he would like to discuss. Be sure to briefly review each of the following areas, all of which have been repeatedly the subjects of recovery tasks:

Telephone Therapy

Has the client been making any telephone contacts? How has that been going?

If the client has not made much progress in building a network of contacts via the phone, can this be facilitated in any way at this point, for example, through role-playing?

Sponsorship

Has the client made any progress toward getting a sponsor?

Does the client have regular contact with the sponsor? In general, does she or he seem to respect this person? Most important, would she or he be likely to follow the sponsor's advice in a time of crisis?

Treatment Note: Facilitating Sponsorship

Getting a sponsor and developing a relationship with that person has been found to correlate with success in recovery from addiction (Sheeren, 1988), and it is probably equally important for a significant other's efforts to move toward caring detachment. If the client has still not approached a sponsor at this point in this program, explore this issue once again. Try to identify and, if possible, work through resistances to initiating contact with a sponsor. The following questions may be useful in such a discussion:

What kind of person would you want to have as a sponsor?

What could you stand to gain from a relationship with a sponsor?

Are you willing to give sponsorship a try, say for 6 months?

What could we do together to make it possible for you to take that first step and say at a meeting that you're looking for a sponsor or else ask someone if they'd think about sponsoring you?

Readings

Has the client read any Al-Anon or Nar-Anon literature? What reactions or questions does she or he have?

Did the client read either the Hazelden pamphlet *Detaching With Love* (Carolyn W., 1984), or the Al-Anon (n.d.) pamphlet *So You Love an Alcoholic?* What reactions did she or he have to these readings?

▓ New Material

Assessing the Client's Commitment to Fellowship

By this time, it is hoped, the client has attended a number of Al-Anon or Nar-Anon meetings and could be said to have at least been exposed to a 12-step fellowship. However, the goal here is to go beyond mere exposure and to facilitate the client's bonding to an Al-Anon or Nar-Anon group. It can be useful for the therapist to take some time now to explore with the client the extent to which this goal has been achieved, using open-ended questions, such as the following:

How would you describe your reaction to the Al-Anon or Nar-Anon meetings you have attended so far?

What have you found most useful about meetings? What has been least useful to you?

Who have you been able to identify with? In what ways can you identify with this person (or persons)?

Do you look forward to meetings? Do you think you would continue to go to meetings if I weren't specifically asking you to go?

Do you feel connected to any one Al-Anon or Nar-Anon group, as though you belong there and being there is important to you? If not, what seems to be the stumbling block?

Do you feel you have a good understanding of the concepts of enabling and caring detachment at this point? Do you have any questions about them?

Surrender

One is often apt to hear, at Al-Anon and Nar-Anon meetings, members urging one another to "turn over" the addict or alcoholic. Such statements refer to the concept of surrender, which derives from the second and third of the 12 steps.

Behaviorally, surrender has to do with a willingness to stop relating to the substance abuser in ways that shield him or her from the natural consequences of substance abuse and that serve to maintain the status quo in the addict-codependent relationship and to accept instead the need to let the substance abuser face life straight on, including taking responsibility for making choices between continuing substance abuse (and its consequences) versus recovery.

Spiritually, surrender challenges significant others to have faith: that allowing the substance abuser to find his or her own way is truly the best course of action in the long run, for the addict, for the significant other, and for their relationship. *By surrendering, the client relieves himself or herself of responsibility, first for causing and now for curing the addiction.*

By enabling addicts (in most cases, for years), significant others unwittingly work to shield the substance abuser and preserve a status quo in the addict-codependent relationship that, ironically, is conducive to maintaining addiction. Many codependents can readily see this, yet the idea of letting go and allowing the addict to experience the natural consequences of substance abuse is fraught with anxieties. For many, the prospect of detaching—this notion of turning over the addict to his or her fate, unfettered, as it were—requires an enormous leap of faith. That is where the second and third steps become particularly relevant for many significant others' struggles to alter their relationships with the addicts. These steps state the following:

Came to believe that a Power greater than ourselves could restore us to sanity.

Made a decision to turn our will and our lives over to the care of God as we understood Him. (Al-Anon, 1985, p. 236)

For some, the ideas expressed in Steps 2 and 3 will pose little or no problem. For one thing, they may already believe in a Higher Power of some sort to whom they turn for comfort and whom they can turn to again as they begin to detach and turn over the alcoholic or addict. Second, they may have bonded to Al-Anon or Nar-Anon and be willing to turn to others as their Higher Power for support as they detach.

In exploring surrender, it can be helpful to ask the client if she or he believes in a God and, if so, if she or he ever prays. In other words, is prayer a source of comfort for the client? Is it something that he or she could turn to now as he or she contemplate detaching from the substance abuser? Many clients can relate to the slogan, "Let go and let God," which implies replacing their own willpower with faith in a Higher Power to lead the addict toward recovery. This frees up the significant other to take care of his or her own needs while changing the way he or she relates to the addict in a fundamental way—to move the relationship from one based on guilt and dependency toward one based on mutual respect and interdependence. Faced with such a profound change in his or her relationship with the enabler, many an addict has eventually made a decision to change and to embrace the 12-step program of AA and NA as a basis for recovery.

Treatment Note: Discussing Personal Spiritual Beliefs

Steps 2 and 3, once again, may tempt the therapist to discuss the client's personal religious beliefs. The issue of spirituality has been brought up earlier, and you may want to review that material again prior to bringing up this topic here. Keep in mind that although as a therapist, you are no doubt a skilled mental health professional, you may not be skilled, trained, or even necessarily experienced in discussing spiritual issues. Moreover, some practitioners may be uncomfortable revealing their personal spiritual beliefs, whereas others may be uncomfortable with certain beliefs. It is sufficient for the therapist to simply point out that 12-step fellowships are nondogmatic in their advocacy of spiritual belief (i.e., they do not define the Higher Power that one is asked to believe in). As has been stated before, it is entirely appropriate to make the fellowship itself (Al-Anon or Nar-Anon) one's Higher Power.

Clients who reject any concept of God, prayer, or both are not to be criticized, much less subjected to any effort on the part of the therapist to change their beliefs. These persons are as capable of surrender as any religious or spiritual person. They merely need to find some form of support in their efforts to detach.

Slogans

"Turn It Over;" "Let Go and Let God;" "Came to Believe;" "One Day at a Time:" These are some of the sayings that the newcomer to a 12-step fellowship is likely to hear repeatedly in meetings. In one way or another, they all relate back to this idea of surrender. They are more than pithy sayings or bumper sticker psychology. They represent a succinct way of keeping the message of Al-Anon and Nar-Anon clear—of keeping the goal in focus.

Surrender may seem like a simple concept, but it is no simple task. As any parent who has let go of a child as he or she became an adult can attest, it is not always easy. So it is with letting go of an addict whose judgment and capacity for making decisions seems to their loved ones to be clearly impaired.

Slogans support surrender. Many are statements of spiritual faith, as when an Al-Anon or Nar-Anon member speaks of letting go and letting God, meaning that a Higher Power will now assume responsibility for the addict instead of the significant other. Such statements of faith can help a great deal when a spouse or other loved one is faced with the challenge of breaking long-standing and entrenched patterns of protecting the addict and taking responsibility for him or her.

"Turning it over" can be taken not only as a statement of spiritual faith but also as a statement of practical wisdom regarding the limits of any adult's responsibility for the decisions and behavior of another. It is common wisdom within Al-Anon and Nar-Anon that codependents tend to feel overly responsible for their partners' substance use. They believe on some level that either they caused or at least contributed to the problem or that they can somehow resolve it. Most harbor underlying fears that detaching will lead to disaster. The long-term impact of their beliefs that they either caused or can cure the problems—especially as their efforts repeatedly fail—include all the symptoms associated with depression: fatigue, hopelessness, low self-esteem, declining health, and so on.

Since their inception, Al-Anon and Nar-Anon have recognized the personal devastation associated with codependence. In their wisdom, these fellowships also recognize just how difficult it can be for people to let go of trying to control addiction in a loved one. They are guided by a strong tradition of providing support for members as they gradually turn over the fate of the addicts in the belief that this is the best course of action and ultimately, a loving thing to do.

Assessing Progress

The therapist should now take some time to explore how the client relates to slogans such as those cited earlier and also to assess how much progress is being made thus far toward turning over the alcoholic or addict to a Higher Power—for example, by not interfering with the natural consequences of his or her substance abuse. Use the foregoing material as a guideline for discussion, along with open-ended questions such as the following:

> Have you heard the expression, "Turn It Over?" How about "Let Go and Let God?" or "Came to Believe?" What do these expressions mean to you, in terms of your relationship with _____?
>
> What do you think you would need to do, concretely, to feel OK about turning it over, in the sense of allowing him or her to be responsible for his or her own actions and their consequences and trusting that this is the best thing you can do for both of you?
>
> What internal resistances do you think you still have to turning over _____'s substance use problem in the way just stated? For example, would you feel anxious? Guilty?

Walking the Walk

To members of 12-step fellowships, the expression "walking the walk" is a familiar and highly meaningful one. In the area of psychotherapy, this same concept has been written about using the more technical phrase, surrender versus compliance in therapy (Tiebout, 1953). In either case, the basic concept is the same and has to do with the extent to which the individual is committed to a program of recovery and bonded to Al-Anon or Nar-Anon versus merely attending meetings. The latter could be called passive involvement and is associated with what is called talking the talk. The former alternative—commitment and bonding—reflects true active involvement. This is what is meant by walking the walk.

From the perspective of those who truly walk the walk of recovery, the merely compliant individual—one who may attend Al-Anon meetings but who does not participate actively in the fellowship—is not likely to surrender or to experience the maximum benefits that commitment offers.

Compliant individuals may go to meetings, but they don't open up, don't develop a network of contacts, don't get a sponsor, don't volunteer for service work, and so forth. In a word, they don't bond. As a result, they may also have difficulty giving up their enabling behaviors and attitudes, because they will lack the ongoing support to do so as well the faith in the wisdom and effectiveness of caring detachment.

Talking the talk, in 12-step terms, is the opposite of walking the walk. Often it amounts to little more than going through the motions, perhaps to placate you, the therapist. It is, in a word, mere compliance. If this is the case, then it is reasonable to expect that the client will revert to old ways of relating to the addict once treatment is terminated.

Initially, the therapist asked nothing more of the client than to give Al-Anon or Nar-Anon a try. Now is an appropriate time to press the issue of whether the client is ready and willing to move beyond mere compliance—beyond talking the talk—to the level of commitment to Al-Anon or Nar-Anon as a vehicle for personal growth, as a viable way of coping with the formidable task of being in a relationship with an addict, and for moving the addict-codependent relationship in a healthier direction. In short, is he or she ready to walk the walk?

Surrender involves a willingness to become truly active and involved in Al-Anon or Nar-Anon, as opposed to merely looking in from the outside, as one significant other put it. The therapist should make this distinction clear and then should ask the client to think about how much she or he is willing to trust Al-Anon or Nar-Anon, to adopt its philosophy, and to embrace the 12-step program as a pathway to recovery for himself or herself. Toward this end, the therapist might ask the client the following questions:

How committed are you at this point to regularly attending Al-Anon or Nar-Anon meetings?

Do you make use of Al-Anon or Nar-Anon literature in helping you to learn to detach?

Do you cultivate a network of Al-Anon or Nar-Anon friends that you talk to regularly?

Sponsorship

Another step toward commitment and bonding comes when the significant other gets a sponsor and communicates regularly with that person. If the client has not as yet gotten a sponsor, address the issue again, now, in the context of this idea of surrender. Using the expression, walking the walk, ask whether the client is now willing to pursue the matter of selecting a temporary Al-Anon or Nar-Anon sponsor. If necessary, clarify again the following regarding the role of the sponsor:

> Sponsors should be individuals of the same sex as the client who have been active in Al-Anon or Nar-Anon for a minimum of 1 year.
>
> Sponsors have sponsors of their own.
>
> Sponsors are not therapists and do not pretend to be.
>
> Sponsors offer sound advice about how to work the 12 steps of Al-Anon and Nar-Anon and how to move from enabling toward caring detachment.

Surrender and Release

So far, this session has focused mostly on some of the cognitive and behavioral facets of surrender. What has been mentioned but not fully explored as yet is the emotional impact associated with surrender.

It has been pointed out that the loved ones of addicts and alcoholics, be they parents, spouses, or siblings, often carry a burden of guilt and shame. Many feel, on some level, that they somehow caused or at least contributed to the substance abuse problem. They feel shame that this disease has been cast on them. Wives in particular are apt to feel these things, because our society continues to place the major responsibility for relationships on women.

As addiction progresses and the relationship between the loved one and the addict gives way to the addict's relationship with alcohol or drugs, jealousy leads to resentment and eventually to alienation and low self-esteem in the significant other. The spiritual well-being of codependents, including their outlook on life, their approach to relationships, and their faith, declines steadily as addiction progresses.

Surrender, like caring detachment, is something that is best approached as a process. However, at some point, many significant others report an experience not unlike a spiritual awakening. This appears to come when they have the clear realization that they can and should let go of their old way of relating to the substance abuser. Associated with this realization is a profound sense of release: release from guilt and shame, to be sure, but also from the stress and anxiety that come from being chronically vigilant, of trying to protect an addict from the consequences of his or her decisions, and of trying to substitute one's own will for that of another.

The sense of relief that comes from letting go of guilt and responsibility for someone else's decisions and behavior and feeling free instead to begin to focus on one's own needs is powerful indeed. It has been described to me using terms ranging from the relatively mild—invigorating—to words that conjure up images of a profound shift in perception of self and others. Hearing people relate such experiences helps one to appreciate more fully the 12th and last step of the

12-step program: "Having had a spiritual awakening as the results of these steps, we tried to carry this message to alcoholics [codependents], and to practice these principles in all our affairs" (AA, 1976, p. 60).

Summing Up

The therapist should once more take a couple of minutes to ask the client to summarize in his or her own words what he or she has gotten out of this session. Particular attention should be paid to getting the client's honest response to how willing he or she is at this time to commit to Al-Anon or Nar-Anon and the 12-step program. Reluctance to totally commit should not be challenged; rather, clarify the client's reasons for this. Keep in mind that thus far, you have primarily asked the client only to give Al-Anon or Nar-Anon a try and that you are now pressing for a greater commitment. The client may indeed need some time to stop and think about this.

Recovery Tasks

Suggested recovery tasks for this topic are as follows:

Meetings

Continue to specifically encourage and reinforce attendance at Al-Anon or Nar-Anon meetings. Be sure to ask how connected the client feels to certain Al-Anon or Nar-Anon groups and members and whether she or he has decided on a home meeting yet. If the client says that she or he does not yet feel connected, suggest that she or he continue going to meetings with the agenda of listening and trying to identify with at least parts of others' experiences, because identification is where bonding begins.

Readings

The following are suggested as appropriate readings for this topic of surrender:

Al-Anon Faces Alcoholism (Al-Anon, 1985), pages 125-131: "A Return to Faith by Way of Al-Anon"

Caring Detachment

As in previous sessions, end by working collaboratively with the client to come up with one or two specific things he or she can do to begin to decrease his or her enabling of the substance abuser and increase caring detachment.

CHAPTER 15

Topic 9

Termination

THE TERMINATION SESSION of this program, like the introductory session, has its own unique format. The primary goal of this final session is to allow the therapist and client, together, to process the client's experiences in the program. A second goal is to assess the client's plans for future action. The therapist encourages continuing involvement in Al-Anon or Nar-Anon.

Treatment Note: On Client-Therapist Bonding

Clinical experience with this program suggests that some clients may become quite bonded to the therapist over time. This is understandable, of course, and happens frequently in any counseling relationship. It is more likely to happen here if the client has made less use of Al-Anon or Nar-Anon than of the therapist in his or her efforts to detach from the substance abuser. The experienced therapist will have anticipated this, will have perceived this bonding as it progressed, and will have brought it—and the reasons for it—into the open for discussion.

A major rationale for systematically encouraging Al-Anon or Nar-Anon involvement throughout this program, of course, has been to prevent excessive reliance on the therapist. Still, despite such efforts, some clients may, in fact, feel dependent on the therapist for their continued recovery.

Though many clients accept the reality of termination with equanimity, it is not that unusual for a client to ask to continue to see the therapist and sometimes, to express considerable anxiety about termination. If this happens, it is recommended that the therapist offer the client any one of the following options:

> To be available to the client *occasionally* via telephone (but not regularly, and not for one-to-one counseling)
>
> To offer one or two booster sessions at 1-month intervals following termination
>
> To offer a follow-up of a few sessions 6 months after termination

The rationale for offering only these options is to encourage the client to use and bond with Al-Anon or Nar-Anon, as opposed to the therapist, as his or her primary resource for recovery.

Program Assessment

In all likelihood, different clients will have found different parts of this program more or less helpful. Recognizing this fact and sharing that expectation with the client at the outset of this last session will encourage honesty in giving feedback to the therapist.

The following is presented as a guideline for helping significant others evaluate their experiences in this program. The therapist should be careful not to rush through this material and might even take notes of the client's comments.

Attitudes Toward Alcoholism and Addiction

> Does the client now believe that he or she can somehow control his or her loved one's use of alcohol or drugs?
>
> At this point, does the client feel responsible in any way for causing his or her partner's substance use?
>
> How does the client understand the concept of denial as it applies to the addict? How does he or she understand it as it applies to himself or herself?
>
> How has the client enabled the addict?
>
> What is the client's understanding of caring detachment and what progress, if any, has he or she made in moving from enabling toward detaching?

Attitudes Toward Al-Anon or Nar-Anon

> What was the client's view of Al-Anon or Nar-Anon prior to treatment, and what is it now?

What has been the client's experience with each of the following with respect to their helpfulness?

Going to meetings

Getting a sponsor

Readings

Telephone therapy

Establishing a network of Al-Anon or Nar-Anon friends

Sponsorship

Journaling

Based on his or her experience, would the client recommend Al-Anon or Nar-Anon to a friend who confided that he or she had a loved one who had an alcohol or drug problem?

What are the client's plans regarding Al-Anon or Nar-Anon involvement for the immediate future?

Attitudes Toward the Treatment Program

Feedback from the client about what he or she found most and least useful about his or her experience with this program provides an opportunity for the therapist to continually enhance his or her clinical expertise. Ask the client for his or her thoughts on each of the following:

What were the most useful parts of this treatment program?

What were the least useful parts of this program?

What is the most important idea or ideas that the client got from these sessions?

If the client could change any part of this program, what would that change be?

Would the client recommend this program to other significant others of substance abusers? What would he or she say about it to such persons?

It is hoped that a thorough and frank discussion of questions like the preceding will leave both the therapist and the client with an appreciation for the work that they have done collaboratively over the course of these sessions, along with a sense of where the client will go from here.

▓ Summing Up

This treatment experience would not be complete if the therapist did not finish it by asking the client for his or her bottom-line assessment:

How are *you* different now than you were when we first met?

How is your *relationship* different now than it was at the start of this program?

If change has occurred in one or both, what do you attribute that change to?

If things have not changed, could that be because the status quo in your relationship with the substance abuser has not changed since you began this program? If that is the case, what would it take to change the status quo between you and the substance abuser in ways that would free you up to become healthier and happier while letting the substance abuser take more responsibility for himself or herself?

Parting

Although not typically done in psychotherapy, it is not inappropriate in this kind of intervention for the therapist and the client to exchange tokens of regard for one another as well as to commemorate the start of the client's recovery, if they choose to do so. Appropriate mementos include Al-Anon or Nar-Anon medallions, greeting cards, meditation books, and so forth. These are readily available today through bookstores.

If the therapist and the client elect to part in such a manner, this should of course be discussed and planned in advance.

Whether or not they choose to celebrate the end of this program with some ritual, though, it is important to part on good terms. Recovery, for codependents and addicts alike, is much like the proverbial journey that is taken a single step at a time. The very fact that the significant other has chosen to complete this program represents one such step for the significant other and in that sense, it cannot be a failure.

Resource: Suggested Reading

THE FOLLOWING IS A LIST of organizations that can be contacted in order to obtain the various readings that have been recommended in this program as well as some additional suggested readings.

Al-Anon

Publications:

Al-Anon Faces Alcoholism (Al-Anon, 1985)
One Day At A Time In Al-Anon (Al-Anon, 1986)
So You Love An Alcoholic (Al-Anon, n.d.)
Understanding Ourselves and Alcoholism (Al-Anon, 1979)

Address:

Al-Anon Family Group Headquarters
One Park Ave.
New York, NY 10159-0182

Alcoholics Anonymous

Publications:

Alcoholics Anonymous, Third Edition (AA, 1976)
Living Sober (AA, 1975)
Twelve Steps and Twelve Traditions (AA, 1952)

Address:

Alcoholics Anonymous World Services
P.O. Box 459
Grand Central Station, NY 10163

Narcotics Anonymous

Publications
Narcotics Anonymous (NA, 1985)
Am I An Addict? (NA, 1983)
Address:
World Services Office, Inc.
P.O. Box 9999
Van Nuys, CA 91409

Hazelden Educational Materials

Publications:
Detaching With Love (Carolyn W., 1984)
Day By Day (Hazelden, 1974)
Twenty-Four Hours A Day (Hazelden, 1954)
Address:
Hazelden Educational Materials
Pleasant Valley Road
P.O. Box 176
Center City, MN 55012-0176

References

Al-Anon. (1979). *Understanding ourselves and alcoholism.* New York: Al-Anon Family Group Headquarters.

Al-Anon. (1985). *Al-Anon faces alcoholism* (2nd ed.). New York: Al-Anon Family Group Headquarters.

Al-Anon. (1986). *One day at a time in Al-Anon.* New York: Al-Anon Family Group Headquarters.

Alcoholics Anonymous. (1952). *Twelve steps and twelve traditions.* Alcoholics Anonymous World Services.

Alcoholics Anonymous. (1975). *Living sober.* New York: Alcoholics Anonymous World Services.

Alcoholics Anonymous. (1976). *Alcoholics anonymous: The story of how many thousands of men and women have recovered from alcoholism* (3rd ed.). New York: Alcoholics Anonymous World Services.

Bellah, R. N., Madsen, W. M., Sullivan, A., Swidler, A., & Tipton, S. M. (1985). *Habits of the heart: Individualism and commitment in American life.* Berkeley: University of California Press.

Bill W. (1992, February). *Tradition two.* New York: The Grapevive (P.O. Box 1980, Grand Central Station, NY). (Original material printed January 1948)

Carolyn W. (1984). *Detaching with love.* Center City, MN: Hazelden.

Collins R. L., Leonard K. E., & Searles J. S. (1990). *Alcohol and the family: Research and clinical perspectives.* New York: Guilford.

Dick Young Productions. (1988). *Family matters* (video). (Available through Hazelden Publications, PO Box 11, Center City, MN.)

Dominguez, T. P., Miller W. R., & Meyers R. J. (1995). *Unilateral intervention with family members of problem drinkers.* Albuquerque: University of New Mexico, Center for Alcoholism, Substance Abuse, and Addictions.

Fowler, J. W. (1993). Alcoholics Anonymous and faith development. In B. S. McCrady & W. R. Miller (Eds.), *Research on Alcoholics Anonymous: Opportunities and alternatives,* (pp. 113-135). New Brunswick, NJ: Rutgers University.

Institute of Medicine. (1990). *Broadening the base of treatment for alcohol problems.* Washington, DC: National Academy Press.

Kurtz, E. (1988). *AA: The story.* New York: Hazelden.

Marlatt, G. A., & Gordon, J. R. (Eds.). (1985). *Relapse prevention.* New York: Guilford.

Marlatt, G. A., Tucker, J. A., Donovan, D. M., & Vuchinich, R. E. (1997). Help-seeking by substance abusers: The role of harm reduction and behavioral-economic approaches to facilitate treatment entry and retention. In L. S. Onken, J. D. Blaine, & J. J. Boren (Eds.), *Beyond the therapeutic alliance: Keeping the drug-dependent individual in treatment* (NIDA Research Monograph 165) (pp. 44-84). Rockville, MD: U.S. Department of Health and Human Services.

Mary M. (1985). *Family denial.* Center City, MN: Hazelden.

McCrady, B. S., & Epstein, E. E. (1996). Theoretical bases of family approaches to substance abuse treatment. In F. Rotgers, D. S. Keller, & J. Morgenstern (Eds.), *Treating substance abuse: Theory and technique* (pp. 125-145). New York: Guilford.

Meyers, R. J, Dominguez, T. P., & Smith, J. E. (1996). Community reinforcement training with concerned others. In V. B. Van Hasselt & M. Hersen (Eds.), *Sourcebook of psychological treatment manuals for adult disorders.* New York: Plenum.

Meyers, R. J., & Smith, J. E. (1995). *Clinical guide to alcohol treatment: The community reinforcement approach.* New York: Guilford.

Miller W. R., & Meyers, R. J. (1994). *Clinical trial of interventions with significant others* (NIAAA Grant No. R01AA09774-01A1.) Albuquerque: University of New Mexico, Center for Alcoholism, Substance Abuse, and Addictions.

Miller W. R., & Meyers, R. J. (1996). *Unilateral family intervention for drug problems: Stage two trial* (NIDA Grant No. R01DA08896-01). Albuquerque: University of New Mexico, Center for Alcoholism, Substance Abuse and Addictions.

Narcotics Anonymous. (1983). *Am I An Addict?* Van Nuys, CA: Narcotics Anonymous World Service Office (P.O. Box 9999, Van Nuys, CA 91409).

Narcotics Anonymous. (1985). *Narcotics Anonymous* (4th ed.). Van Nuys, CA: Narcotics Anonymous World Service Office.

National Institute on Drug Abuse. (1995, June). *National household survey on drug abuse, main findings 1993* (DHHS Publication [SMA] 95-3020). U.S. Department of Health and Human Services.

Nowinski, J. (1990). *Substance abuse in adolescents and young adults: A guide to treatment.* New York: Norton.

Nowinski, J. (in press). Self-help groups. In B. S. McCrady & E. E. Epstein (Eds.), *Addictions: A comprehensive guidebook for practitioners.* New York: Oxford University Press.

Nowinski, J., Baker, S., & Carroll, K. (1992). *Twelve-step facilitation therapy manual.* (Project MATCH Monograph series, vol. 1.) Rockville, MD: National Institute on Alcohol Abuse and Alcoholism.

Nowinski, J., & Baker, S. (1998). *The twelve-step facilitation handbook.* San Francisco: Jossey-Bass. (Originally published 1992)

Paolino, T. J., & McCrady, B. S. (1977). *The alcoholic marriage: Alternative perspectives.* New York: Grunne & Stratton.

Prochaska, J. O., DiClemente, C. C., & Norcross, J. C. (1992). In search of how people change: Applications to addictive behaviors. *American Psychologist, 47,* 9.

Room, R. (1993). Alcoholics Anonymous as a social movement. In B. S. McCrady & W. R. Miller (Eds.), *Research on Alcoholics Anonymous: Opportunities and alternatives.* New Brunswick, NJ: Rutgers University Press.

Sheeren, M. (1988). The relationship between relapse and involvement in Alcoholics Anonymous. *Journal of Studies on Alcohol, 49,* 104-106.

So You Love An Alcoholic. (n.d.). Midtown Station, NY: Al-Anon Family Group Headquarters.

Solberg, R.J. (1983). *The dry drunk syndrome.* Center City, MN: Hazelden.

Thomas, E. J., & Ager, R. D. (1993, June). *Characteristics of unmotivated alcohol abusers and their spouses.* Paper presented at the Research Society on Alcoholism, Annual Meeting, San Antonio, TX.

Tiebout, H. M. (1953). Surrender versus compliance in therapy. *Quarterly Journal of Studies on Alcohol, 14,* 58-68. (Available through Hazelden Educational Materials, Center City, MN.)

Index

181

About the Author

Joseph K. Nowinski, PhD, is Associate Adjunct Professor of Psychology at the University of Connecticut and supervising psychologist at the University of Connecticut Correctional Managed Care Unit. Dr. Nowinski has consulted for Yale University and the National Institute on Alcohol Abuse and Alcoholism on Project MATCH, a national collaborative study of treatment for alcohol abuse, and the Center on Substance Abuse, Alcoholism and Addiction of the University of New Mexico on studies of treatment of significant others of substance abusers. He has developed treatment programs for substance abusers and their significant others. He is the author of *Substance Abuse in Adolescents and Young Adults: A Guide to Treatment* and coauthor of *The Twelve-Step Facilitation Handbook.* He lives in Tolland, Connecticut.